Foreword

The launching of an earth satellite by the Soviet Union in October 1957 brought the American people abruptly to a realization of the advanced technical and scientific capacities which now stand behind the threatening posture of the Soviet Union toward the free world.

Earlier, in 1953, following the death of Premier Stalin, the new leadership of the Kremlin had launched a different and unannounced offensive against the free nations—a massive program of trade, aid, and technical assistance aimed at the world's less developed countries. The nature of the major aid agreements which the Sino-Soviet bloc has concluded with these "target" countries and the intensity with which the bloc has pursued its trade-aid campaign in the last 3 years have helped to underscore the statement of Nikita Khrushchev, now Premier of the U.S.S.R., who declared in 1955: "We value trade least for economic reasons and most for political purposes."

It is of great importance that the American people, now well aware of the technical and scientific challenge posed by the Communist world, understand and rise to meet the equally great, and perhaps more subtly dangerous, offensive which the Sino-Soviet bloc has vigorously launched in the less developed areas. This offensive represents an attempt by the Sino-Soviet bloc to employ its growing economic and industrial capacities as a means for bringing the newly developing free nations within the Communist orbit.

The facts presented in this document reveal the dimensions of the Sino-Soviet economic offensive in the less developed countries. The document does not pretend to set forth answers to the problems which confront us, but is limited rather to a description of the scope and nature of the offensive and an analysis of its motives and objectives. This paper was prepared by the Department of State on the basis of a careful study of material available from a great many different sources.

DOUGLAS DILLON,
Deputy Under Secretary of State for Economic Affairs

The SINO-SOVIET ECONOMIC OFFENSIVE in the LESS DEVELOPED COUNTRIES

GREENWOOD PRESS, PUBLISHERS
NEW YORK

Originally published in 1958
Washington, D.C.

First Greenwood Reprinting 1969

Library of Congress Catalogue Card Number 70-90729

SBN 8371-2270-8

PRINTED IN UNITED STATES OF AMERICA

Contents

List of Tables

Page

Introduction

"If the purpose of Soviet aid to any country were simply to help it overcome economic difficulties without infringing its freedom, such aid could be welcomed as forwarding the free world purpose of economic growth. But there is nothing in the history of international communism to indicate this can be the case. Until such evidence is forthcoming, we and other free nations must assume that Soviet bloc aid is a new, subtle, and long-range instrument directed toward the same old purpose of drawing its recipient away from the community of free nations and ultimately into the Communist orbit."—Dwight D. Eisenhower, in his message to Congress, February 19, 1958.

. . . .

Communists have never abandoned their ultimate goal, which is world domination. They have shifted emphasis from one course to another, but always their strategy and tactics, even though apparently inconsistent or contradictory, have clearly been directed toward achieving the objective set for them by Lenin more than 40 years ago.

First they concentrated on gaining control of a state where conditions offered them an excellent opportunity: Russia. They were working even then, however, to dominate other countries, and after consolidating their power in the Soviet Union they went on to other areas. Eastern Europe first fell to their control—10 countries, one by one.

This was accomplished by both political and military action. Subversion was employed in advance. Hard-core Communist groups were ready to assume political control when the moment came. China was the next to come under the international Communists' control, and again the same pattern of preparation was evident—the hard core of Lenin's disciples, subversion of influential groups, political action, military action, all employed according to what was most expedient and promising at any particular time.

In 1950 the Communists launched direct and open aggression against Korea, which was met by an immediate and ultimately successful effort by the United States and its free-world allies to check this aggression. Since then the Communists have come to place more and more reliance on a wider and wider range of nonmilitary tactics for accomplishing their expansionist goals. This does not mean that they have devoted less effort to building up their military might. Quite the contrary. But it does indicate that the Communists feel that they stand greater chance of success, while avoiding unacceptable risks of war, through placing greater emphasis upon economic and political subversion.

The new tactic, economic penetration, is the most dangerous of all. The story of this economic tactic is the subject of the document that follows.

Part One

Bloc Objectives, Capabilities, and Methods

I. THE SETTING IN THE LESS DEVELOPED AREAS

The Soviet economic offensive is carefully shaped to exploit the aspirations as well as the dissatisfactions of the less developed countries of the free world. While average per capita income in the less developed areas varies widely from country to country, the bulk of the people continue to live in extreme poverty, which was generally accepted as inevitable in the past. This attitude no longer predominates. The postwar period has witnessed a remarkable upsurge of hope and determination to achieve modernization and economic growth—aptly called by one prominent scholar "the revolution of rising expectations." Throughout the world, governments of the less developed countries are committed as a matter of the highest priority to industrialization and the expansion of production. The drive is related primarily to the desire of the average man for more material welfare and to the political demands upon governments which this creates.

In general, these countries have set for themselves ambitious development goals which exceed their own resources in capital as well as technical and entrepreneurial skills. They face particular difficulties in trying to achieve the rapid industrialization on which they place such a high premium as a symbol of economic independence. A significant number of political parties or groups consider that centralized planning and substantial participation of the state in investment programs is essential to their rapid economic growth. While many of these people may be opposed to Communist political institutions and methods, they are frequently impressed by Soviet industrial growth and technological achievements, although these have yet to attain previous Western European and North American levels.

Most governments recognize that development must depend largely on the country's own efforts, but they also feel that foreign economic assistance is indispensable to rapid growth and they therefore actively seek capital and technical assistance from abroad. At the same time they maintain a zealous guard against any economic commitments which they consider might impair their sovereignty.

There is widespread readiness in the less developed countries—particularly those with a colonial past—to attribute their poverty to their previous political status. Communist propaganda plays heavily on this theme by misrepresenting United States trade and aid programs as merely a new disguise for the old "imperialism" designed to maintain the nonindustrial countries in a state of economic subjugation. Where prejudice is strong, such distortions have gained acceptance among some groups. However, antiwesternism and readiness to blame current frustrations on the West are not necessarily synonymous with a pro-Communist attitude or naiveté regarding Soviet and Communist Chinese political ambitions. While leaders of a few of the less developed countries may overestimate their ability to control the threat from the bloc, the majority recognize the advantages of free-world trade and assistance and would accept a serious degree of economic entanglement with the bloc, if at all, only as a last resort.

In this context, the ability of the less developed countries to dispose readily of their exports at stable prices in traditional free-world markets is important. Most of these countries are heavily dependent on export earnings from a few primary commodities to finance imports essential not only to development but also to the maintenance of current consumption. Thus, if markets for these commodities should contract as a result of substantially reduced demand or restrictionist commercial policies in the developed countries, the disadvantages of large-scale bilateral trading with the bloc would lose much of their force as deterrents to the acceptance of bloc trade and aid overtures.

Other factors of a more strictly political character also play a major role in determining the foreign economic relations of the less developed countries. While the situation in each country has unique aspects, certain elements are common to most cases. The outstanding example is intense nationalism, which usually explains the zeal to reduce dependence on the industrialized countries and which inspires many governmental actions on the part of the less developed countries—particularly the newly independent nations of Asia and Africa—regardless of adverse economic consequences.

Such uneconomic measures and the resulting institutional disturbances contribute to internal political unrest; they also affect the ability and even the willingness of the Western countries to contribute to the badly needed economic development of these areas. Yet the governments of the less developed countries are under constant pressures to take measures which give the appearance of hastening internal economic advancement. Under these circumstances some have undertaken to obtain economic aid from both East and West, counting on the willingness of the great powers to bid for such opportunities.

Neutralism has been another major political factor affecting the bloc's willingness and ability to pursue its economic offensive in the free world. As a political idea, neutralism originally implied ideological detachment from both the Soviet bloc and the free world. In recent years, however, emphasis has been given to detachment from the West, and the term "positive neutralism" has been coined in the Afro-Asian area to convey this anti-Western shade of meaning. From the point of view of Soviet propaganda, neutralism is exploited not as an isolationist detachment from the bloc as well as the West, but as a *rapprochement* with the Soviet bloc.

The practice of neutralism is far from uniform among the Afro-Asian countries and depends both on their historical involvement and their problems in current relations with the major powers. At best, it takes the form of efforts by the more prominent leaders to play impartial intermediary roles to reduce world tensions between the bloc and the free world or to make appeals to both the U.S.S.R. and the West to stop nuclear weapons tests and manufacture. In the extreme, it manifests itself in regional solidarity demonstrations against the West and in attacks upon free-world defense and economic policies. In the economic field, neutralism tends to take the form of expanding relations with the bloc, a course of action which some groups view as not more dangerous to independence than confining such relations to the industrialized nations of the West. Chapters II and IV provide important data bearing on this question.

Disputes between nations and Soviet readiness to aggravate them have also been a major factor influencing some of the less developed countries to expand economic relations with the bloc. When bloc credits in such circumstances include the provision of arms under favorable purchase terms, together with military advisers and technicians, the way is opened to deeper involvement. Thus the extensive Soviet-bloc economic ties with Egypt, and later Syria, can be related directly to the Arab-Israeli dispute and to bloc provision of arms in support of Egyptian-Syrian military aspirations. Soviet support for Egypt and Syria subsequently moved into the field of large-scale credits for economic development. The political dispute between Afghanistan and Pakistan is another example of a situation in which the Soviets, by supporting Afghanistan, took advantage of local rivalry. More recently, the Soviets have attempted to encourage Yemen's border dispute with the United Kingdom over Aden and the Dutch-Indonesian dispute over Western New Guinea.

By and large, the presence of local Communist parties has not been an important factor in promoting acceptance of economic programs, since the ability of such groups to influence the foreign policies of the government is generally minimal or nonexistent. The same is generally true of "front groups," although in some countries they have had nuisance value to the U.S.S.R. by spreading propaganda that more extensive economic dealings with the bloc would alleviate trade problems and serve to promote nationalist development goals. The Afro-Asian Peoples' Solidarity Conference, which met in Cairo at the end of 1957, was an attempt by the U.S.S.R. to use an international group to promote its economic offensive.

In recent years the strategy of international communism has been to play down the overt relationship of the U.S.S.R. to local Communist movements and has called for the identification of Communist goals with the aspirations of the majority groups. This apparent shift from the earlier strategy of international communism tends to reinforce other elements in the Soviet drive for respectability and, while not always taken at face value, has probably served in some areas to blur the threat of economic ties with the bloc.

II. MOTIVES AND OBJECTIVES

The bloc economic offensive is a major instrument of Soviet foreign policy and reflects its principal objectives. While the European satellites have played a significant role in the offensive in some countries, it is the U.S.S.R. which has determined the overall policy, defined its ideological and political significance, taken the dramatic steps to promote its psychological impact, and engineered the more spectacular deals with the less developed countries.

Motivation Primarily Political

"We value trade least for economic reasons and most for political purposes," Mr. Khrushchev remarked to a group of U.S. Congressmen in 1955. This attitude applies with greatest force to the less developed countries where trade and aid ventures, as an integral part of the "new look" Soviet foreign policy, can yield the largest political returns. The offensive has thus been aimed especially at the "neutralist" countries of Asia and Africa. The nature and circumstances of the major aid agreements concluded by the U.S.S.R. and its more publicized trade operations with these target countries (which are discussed in Part Two) clearly illustrate the use of these weapons in support of Soviet political objectives. The concerted bombardment of trade and aid offers in the last 3 years is more obviously a contrived campaign which could not, of course, be explained by commercial considerations alone. Soviet statements both at home and abroad have, in fact, highlighted the political aspects of the offensive by stressing its importance in "the struggle against imperialism," a favorite Communist propaganda piece.

While the Soviet motivation is overwhelmingly political, the European satellites have a strong economic incentive to participate in the offensive in view of their pressing need for imported primary products and foreign markets for their manufactures (see Chapter III). East Germany, of course, also has the objective of using trade and credits to gain respectability, representation, and eventually diplomatic recognition in nonbloc countries. Even though the impetus to satellite participation is heavily economic, the total weight of their economic presence in the less developed countries adds substantially to Soviet ability to promote its political objectives.

The Peiping regime's participation in the bloc economic offensive is no less politically motivated than is the Soviet Union's. Political purposes are evident in offers of credits and grants by Communist China, itself an underdeveloped area. With respect to trade, Communist China's requirements for raw material exports of the less developed countries are quite limited and its interest in

President Nasser and a Russian engineer view a model of a Soviet oil refinery at an industrial exhibit at Cairo.

promoting trade in that area is often inspired as much by subversive intent as by a need to obtain transferable foreign exchange.

Politically, trade and aid serve as instruments in Communist China's efforts to obtain recognition as the established government of China and ultimately as the great power of Asia. Three of the four countries which have recognized Communist China since the Korean conflict—Nepal, Egypt, and Yemen—have been rewarded with allocations of economic aid. By emphasizing trade and aid as a major facet of its relations with other countries, the Chinese Communists seek to create the image of a friendly and prosperous nation with which relations of mutual benefit can be established or expanded. Together with the U.S.S.R., Communist China seeks to impress less developed countries, particularly in Southeast Asia, with its progress toward industrialization and to recommend its type of planned economy as a model for Asian economic development. In so doing, the affinity as a fellow Asian country which suffered the ills of colonialism is stressed. Despite its limited means, Peiping stands ready to use economic aid, grants as well as credits, for subversive purposes. This was demonstrated by the unsuccessful attempt of Communist forces in Laos in early 1957 to make the acceptance of substantial financial aid from Communist China a condition for a political settlement with the Lao Government.

Thus the motivation of the Soviet Union and Communist China is primarily political, while European satellite motivation is heavily economic. The sum total of the bloc economic offensive, in view of Communist political objectives, is a threat to the less developed countries and their peaceful relations with other free-world nations.

Part of Broader Foreign Policy Considerations

The immediate political objectives and tactics of the U.S.S.R. in its economic offensive vary considerably from country to country. The Soviet Union's purposes in giving economic aid to India and Burma are different from those involved in Egypt and Syria or, for that matter, in Latin America. In other words, the Soviets' objectives would vary with the overall foreign policy objectives which the U.S.S.R. has determined for a given country or area. Economic weapons are used only as one part of the broader, well integrated political campaign aimed at any given target. However, Soviet policy vis-a-vis the less developed countries is sufficiently consistent to permit certain useful generalizations.

Gain in Influence and Goodwill

One of the most important and immediate objectives of the Soviet economic offensive is the desire to establish Soviet influence in the crucial uncommitted areas by acquiring a considerable measure of goodwill, especially among the key, politically articulate groups. This desire of the Soviet leadership to emerge from Stalinist isolationism is heralded by them as a return to Leninist principles of foreign policy, and significantly Soviet literature on the economic offensive has quoted Lenin's statement on identification with the national independence movements of the former colonial territories, viz., "We will apply all our force to become close to and to unite with the Mongols, the Persians, the Indians, and the Egyptians. We consider it to be our obligation and to *our interest* to do this because otherwise socialism in Europe would be unstable." (italics Lenin's)[1]

To accomplish this objective, the Soviet economic deals are fitted into the context of broader political activities in the area, such as espousing and supporting Arab, Indian, Afghan, and Indonesian political objectives. As an immediate accomplishment, the Soviet economic offensive has already introduced thousands of bloc technicians into the less developed countries and brought thousands of technicians from those countries to the U.S.S.R. This in itself is an important step in gaining goodwill and influence and in impressing key groups in these countries with the "friendly and sympathetic" attitude of the U.S.S.R., with the image of the U.S.S.R. as a country supposedly free of racial discrimination (a point of considerable interest in the less developed countries), and with the considerable technological and industrial achievements of the U.S.S.R. under socialism.

---

[1] Lenin, *Sochinenya*, vol. 23, p. 55, quoted in Rubenstein, M., "Several Economic Questions of the Underdeveloped Countries," *World Economy and International Relations*, No. 3, September 1957 (title and name of journal translated from Russian).

Enhanced influence and goodwill gained in this fashion can also be achieved through cultural exchanges, and indeed such a program is actively being carried on by the bloc. But economic aid lends substance to the campaign, which, as a whole, would have been considerably less effective if the vital field of aid to economic development, which is of such dominant concern to these countries, had been left exclusively to the West.

Encouragement of Anti-Western Neutralism

Closely allied with the immediate and general objective of establishing Soviet influence in the target countries and gaining their goodwill are the more specifically anti-Western but equally immediate objectives of encouraging neutralism, lessening Western influence, exacerbating free-world tensions, and undermining free-world alliances and alinements.

The bloc's economic offensive furthers these general goals by making neutralism seem to pay. Bloc economic aid and trade, insofar as they are, or promise to be, beneficial to the recipient country, strengthen the hand of those groups which favor a politically neutralist position or one of closer alinement with the bloc, and counter the arguments of those who point to the economic disruptions and disadvantages which have frequently followed from anti-Western politics. Programs of economic and military assistance have already done much to support Soviet policy in such key countries as Egypt and Syria, where recent events have radically altered the political scene.

The Soviet leaders may consider that it is sufficient that Soviet economic, technical, or military assistance may be available to encourage a country to adopt a specific anti-Western policy or take a specific anti-Western action which would involve economic difficulties. The Egyptian nationalization of the Suez Canal and the Indonesian campaign against Dutch interests are cases in point. It is significant in this connection that at the recent Afro-Asian Peoples' Solidarity Conference at Cairo, the Soviet delegate urged upon the less developed countries a policy of nationalization of foreign interests in the full knowledge, of course, that such action would tend to disturb relations between Western and less developed countries.

At this early date in the bloc offensive, there is no clear evidence that the U.S.S.R. has used its aid to require a recipient country to adopt a specific policy or to take a specific action, as for example, by the threat of the withdrawal of Soviet aid. In most cases the use of the economic weapon is more subtle, encouraging the recipient to adopt positions or take actions which would otherwise be too costly or dangerous. This has been especially true in the Arab countries. In other areas, such as Latin America, where the U.S.S.R. cannot reasonably have hoped to change materially the basic foreign policy orientation of target countries through its economic offensive, the U.S.S.R. probably will consider its efforts well spent if they serve to increase Soviet respectability and encourage friction in the good relations of these countries with the United States. Thus far, it has been feasible for the Soviet Union to promote anti-Western manifestations of "neutralism" through trade and aid programs, despite the fact that such programs are frequently on a small scale.

Support to Specific Propaganda Objectives

The specific propaganda points which the U.S.S.R. seeks to hammer home to the less developed countries are woven into its economic offensive. In the field of psychological warfare—"the struggle for men's minds"—the U.S.S.R. hopes to use the politically articulate elites of Asia and Africa by posing as the benevolently disinterested "brother" and champion of the less developed countries in their struggles for economic development and "independence" against the alleged machinations of the "imperialist West." Through its economic programs, the bloc seeks to identify itself with the powerful current of nationalism sweeping not only the former colonial regions but also the Latin American countries and to create the impression of Soviet interest in the closely related and no less intense desire of these countries for rapid economic development, particularly industrialization. The governing groups in these countries consider economic improvement to be necessary not only for the solution of internal problems but also for the attainment of greater international status and prestige and have committed their political fortunes to this end. It is apparent that the bloc is striving to channel these powerful forces against the West.

In doing this, the propaganda side of the economic offensive plays on the following deep-rooted sentiments in the less developed countries, and the existing Soviet programs tend to lend credence to the propaganda claim, especially among less sophisticated and biased groups in the target countries.

The Desire for Economic Development and the Rise of Living Standards. This sentiment is generally translated into the desire for industrial development; the factory has become an almost irrational symbol of economic progress in many newly developing countries. Soviet propaganda distorts Western statements about the desirability of balanced growth which emphasize the complementary need for the development of agriculture, natural resources, and other elements of economic progress which may be less spectacular than new manufacturing plants. The U.S.S.R. in its propaganda claims to encourage industrialization and to lend material assistance to its achievement. The thesis is that industrialization, especially "production of the means of production," is the only guaranty of true economic independence of each country. The U.S.S.R. points to its own emergence from backwardness to indicate a supposed community of interest with the less developed countries.

Dissatisfaction With the Terms of Trade. The less developed countries, which are highly dependent on raw materials exports, are frequently dissatisfied with world market prices. The Communists play on this sentiment, portraying the situation as the result of deliberate manipulation by "imperialist monopolies" with the object of maintaining the less developed countries in "slavery" and of preventing them from developing their own industrial production. The Soviet Union, on the other hand, claims that the nature of the Socialist economy is such that it has no inherent need to "subjugate" underdeveloped countries. Consequently, it can offer what it calls "just" prices for raw materials and it can follow up in selected cases with favorable deals when a country is faced with marketing difficulties for its raw materials

(e. g., the Burmese rice and Egyptian cotton deals). On the other hand, it sometimes resells these same commodities in the world market to gain needed convertible exchange. This option will, of course, continue to remain open under the Soviet's state-controlled trading system.

Dissatisfaction With the Terms of Western Aid. Soviet propaganda attacks the interest rates on Western loans and credits which are characterized as a means of "exploiting" the less developed countries and keeping them in "economic bondage." It also plays heavily on the theme that Western economic assistance is accompanied by political strings which infringe the sovereignty of the recipient country. Soviet aid is portrayed, by contrast, as generous in its terms and "without strings" (see Chapter IV). To the extent that the West increases its aid or makes its terms more attractive, Soviet propaganda claims that the change is a reaction to the Soviet's program.

Soviet Economic Prestige. Finally, also in the realm of ideas, the U.S.S.R. through its economic programs seeks to publicize its emergence from relative backwardness to a position of economic power. This is part of a broader campaign designed to emphasize the economic superiority of the Soviet type of economy for rapid development and, at the same time, to underline Soviet overall power. As one Soviet writer put it, the current economic offensive is "a new form of the economic competition between the two systems but one which takes place in the territories of countries having a majority of the human race." [2]

Eventual Communist Domination

The points discussed above refer to the near term or proximate objectives of the bloc's economic offensive. World political domination, of course, remains the ultimate Soviet objective, but the present phase probably does not contemplate early "satellization" of even the principal target countries; and it is unlikely, in any case, that a take-over could be accomplished by strictly economic means. However, to the extent that the bloc becomes a major trading partner or plays an important role in a country's development, it may conceivably bring about such a degree of economic dependence as to create important political leverage. The ability of the Soviets to use economic threats to force a country to take actions against its own desire would be problematical since the nationalist feeling that this would evoke might well be stronger than the weapons employed. The failure of the bloc's economic embargo against Yugoslavia is a case in point. Such overt pressures are particularly apt to be avoided in instances where the bloc feels the country can and will turn to the Western alternatives.

Eventually closer economic ties are expected to facilitate espionage and subversion in target countries in view of the large number of bloc technicians and indoctrination through training, but in most cases the U.S.S.R. and other bloc members have apparently been careful, thus far, to administer their foreign economic activities on a "correct" basis. In the current phase of the offensive any other approach would be counterproductive, and the U.S.S.R. will prob-

---

[2] Rubenstein, *ibid.*

ably be satisfied with attaining interim objectives considerably short of political domination.

The U.S.S.R. evidently expects that close economic ties with the less developed countries will eventually strengthen domestic pressures for Soviet-type governments. Mr. Khrushchev, on the occasion of his Asian trip in November–December of 1955, stressed the superiority of communism as a key to economic development. At the recent Afro-Asian solidarity meeting, the Soviet delegation repeatedly pointed to the U.S.S.R.'s experience in economic development as a model to all less developed countries. It is also significant that virtually all Soviet aid to date has gone into projects for the government-owned sector of the economies of the recipient countries. As one Soviet writer put it:

> The great successes of the socialist countries exert a great influence on the peoples of the underdeveloped countries, strengthen the ideas on authority of socialism among different progressive factors of the population, which have decisively declared themselves against capitalism. In connection with this in many underdeveloped countries there is manifested a striving for the predominant development of state-owned industry as the basis of economic development. . . . The active intervention of the state in economic life creates the prerequisites for a planned economy in the state-owned sector.[3]

And the Soviet view of the possible consequences of this was spelled out by another writer:

> Where will the further development of state ownership of the most important means of production lead—this will depend upon the correlation and struggle of class forces. In certain conditions this may become the material basis for the peaceful transformation to socialism.[4]

Thus the U.S.S.R. probably does not feel compelled to stimulate industrial growth to the point where a politically powerful proletariat would exist to achieve the Socialist revolution. Although the Marxist view is that the revolution will occur in the last stages of industrial capitalism, the Communist take-over has generally come in relatively underdeveloped countries which had only recently embarked on development under capitalism or a mixed economy. The class which the U.S.S.R. is playing for is not the as yet insignificant industrial proletariat in these countries but what the Soviets call the "national bourgeoisie," which is considered to be a potential ally in the vulnerable, early stages of capitalism.

> The national bourgeoisie, to the extent that it is interested in the strengthening and development of sovereign national states cannot but recognize that the countries of the socialist system are actually the hoped for support of their national independence. . . .[5]

It is this politically articulate group which the U.S.S.R. hopes to influence by the economic offensive. Thus Soviet policy of aid to the less developed countries for the accomplishment of proximate advantage in the cold war is not inconsistent with the traditional objectives of Communist revolutions and eventual take-over of the target countries.

---

[3] Osipov, U., "Economic Collaboration of the Countries of the Socialist Camp with the Underdeveloped Countries of Asia and the East," *Financi SSSR*, No. 8, August 1957.

[4] Rubenstein, *op. cit.*

[5] Zhukov, E., "40 Years That Decided the Destiny of Colonialism," *World Economy and International Relations*, No. 4, October 1957.

The "Crisis of Capitalism"

Another important facet of long-range Communist strategy is that of aggravating the "crisis of capitalism." This is an important aspect of Leninism, which is the guiding ideology of the U.S.S.R. According to Leninist theory, the "inevitable downfall of capitalism" is preceded in its last stages by the phenomenon of imperialism. In the struggle to stave off the ultimate collapse brought about by their "internal contradictions" the capitalist countries attempt to acquire colonies, which are an important outlet for surplus capital and production and an indispensable source of raw materials. That is why Lenin advocated the support of "national liberation" movements in the colonies and dependent areas.

In the current Soviet ideology, the loss of colonies by various European nations following World War II is described as both a symptom and a cause of the decline of Western capitalism, a decline which the West is allegedly trying to overcome by attempting to maintain and reassert its economic domination. Insofar as the less developed countries succeed in their attempts to achieve economic independence, it is claimed that the West will be further weakened, both politically and economically. The existence of the Socialist market is characterized as helping the less developed countries to reduce their economic dependence on the West. In this context, anything the bloc does to support these countries or to exacerbate these tensions is considered to "give history a push" in hastening the decline of Western "imperialist" capitalism.

> The disintegration of the colonial system shakes the bases of imperialism. It is a result of the general crisis of capitalism, and in its turn, further deepens this crisis.[6]

---

[6] Varga, E. "Of the Tendencies of Development of Contemporary Capitalism and Socialism," *ibid.*

III. BLOC CAPABILITIES

The U.S.S.R. and other bloc countries undoubtedly have the economic and technological capability to carry out economic assistance programs of considerable scope. They certainly are capable of executing the programs to which they are already committed. And substantial expansion on a selective basis would also be possible without unduly severe strain.

Bloc Economic Growth

The rapid growth of Soviet economic power is a matter of record; future growth is likely to be at a relatively fast rate, even if slower than in the past. In recent years the U.S.S.R. has achieved an average increase of possibly as much as 7 percent yearly in gross national product, which is now estimated at some $170 billion. Of this, industrial production constitutes $68 billion, making the U.S.S.R. the second largest industrial power in the world. Industrial growth has averaged 9 to 10 percent annually in recent years; this will probably decline somewhat in the coming few years, though the industrial product 5 years hence may be 50–60 percent above that of 1957. For the same 5-year period the Soviet gross national product will probably increase by 6 percent annually.

In the East European satellites the rates of growth of GNP and gross industrial production were slightly below those of the U.S.S.R. For 1957 the total GNP generated in the East European area is estimated at some $65–70 billion, with industry contributing approximately 40 percent. Almost 85 percent of the total originated in the three most industrialized countries—Czechoslovakia, East Germany, and Poland. Communist China, with a less developed industrial base, has attained greater percentage increases in production. Even if the claimed 130 percent increase in industrial output for the 5-year period ending in 1957 is discounted as extravagant, there is no doubt that notable advances have been made, particulary in heavy industry. However, Communist China's GNP is on the order of only $40 billion, and its agriculture has barely kept pace with the rapid growth of population.

Though Soviet foreign trade has been increasing rapidly, it is still small enough in relation to total Soviet production to allow the U.S.S.R. to increase substantially its foreign trade without radical changes in the structure of the Soviet economy or in the fundamentals of Soviet economic philosophy. In 1957 total Soviet foreign trade turnover amounted to over $8.25 billion. In 2 years it had increased by 25 percent, and the U.S.S.R. became sixth in rank among the trading nations of the world. However, exports, roughly half of this amount, account for about 2.5 percent of Soviet GNP, still a comparatively low figure (and about one-half of the United States ratio). Over two-thirds of this trade was with the other bloc nations.

The U.S.S.R. and other bloc nations possess, therefore, a potent economic base from which to expand their economic drive in the less developed countries. In view of the importance attached by the U.S.S.R. to this offensive in terms of its expected political rewards, there is no reason to think that the Soviet Union or other bloc countries have come to the end of the road in pushing their credit and trade deals. The U.S.S.R. can certainly sustain the relatively small annual drain implied in its present commitments for assistance, which will be utilized by the recipient over periods as long as 7 years in some cases. It can even substantially increase these. Though additional commitments must be made by the U.S.S.R. on a selective basis, the U.S.S.R. is capable of incurring these, even in cases where they are economically burdensome, to shoot for greater political gains.

Limitations

No country, of course, has unlimited capabilities for economic assistance, and the U.S.S.R. is no exception. Some of these limitations are peculiar to the U.S.S.R., however, and affect the extent to which the U.S.S.R. will be able or likely to push this economic offensive. These limitations bear also in varying degrees on the satellites and Communist China, sometimes less and sometimes more acutely. The enormous burden in terms of men and resources required to develop and maintain the huge Soviet military establishment is the most obvious and important limitation on Soviet capability to engage in foreign economic assistance. Other limitations inhere principally in the great demand for investment goods in the bloc and the consequent limited availability of these products in quantity for export purposes.

Soviet Domestic Demands for Capital Resources

Since the end of the twenties the Soviet economy has been subjected to a forced industrialization, aimed at the most rapid development of the industrial economy and of the military machine which rests upon it. The high rates of industrial growth have, however, declined in recent years, and Soviet plans have recognized this condition. The U.S.S.R. claimed a yearly increase of over 13 percent in industrial output in 1951–55. (This official Soviet figure is higher than the Department of State estimate given above.) The Five-Year Plan for 1956–60 involved a scaling down of the projected yearly increase to less than 11 percent. The annual plan for 1956 called for a 10.5 percent increase and that for 1957 a still further reduction to 7.1 percent. These reductions led to the unprecedented abandonment in September 1957 of the whole Five-Year Plan. The drastic reorganization of industrial management initiated in the spring of 1957 and a succession of radical measures in agriculture testify to the continued concern of Soviet leaders over the decline in growth rates. How successful the Soviet Union will be in maintaining high rates of growth is open to question. It is the up-to-now neglected sectors such as agriculture, housing and civic facilities, consumer-goods manufactures, and transportation that are making new demands on Soviet investment capacities; investment in these sectors is less "reproductive" than investment in heavy industry. The situation has been further complicated by various factors: a manpower shortage stemming from the reduced birth rate during the war years and the commitment to reduce the workweek; by the necessity of exploiting lower grade ores; and by the need to invest in increased amounts to cover replacement of capital equipment owing to insufficient retirement of obsolescent equipment in previous years.

Soviet Aid to Bloc as Limitation on Direct U.S.S.R. Economic Assistance to Underdeveloped Countries

Since 1956 Soviet capabilities for contributing directly to the bloc economic offensive in underdeveloped countries have also been affected by changes in relations with the satellites and by Soviet efforts to reestablish bloc cohesion in Europe. The earlier pattern of economic exploitation of the satellites has been alleviated, so that by 1957 they may have become a net drain on the

TABLE 1. *Soviet Economic Assistance to the Bloc, Calendar Years 1956 and 1957*

(Millions of U.S. dollars) [a]

Recipient countries	Credits					Cancellation of debts	Grants	Other economic assistance
	Total credit	Development credit	Commodity credit	Currency credit	Unspecified credit			
Albania	47.75	40.00	7.75	------	------	105.50	------	------
Bulgaria	142.50	67.50	75.00	------	------	------	------	------
Czechoslovakia	------	------	------	------	------	------	------	------
Communist China [b]	------	------	------	------	------	------	------	------
East Germany	280.00	------	100.00	180.00	------	------	------	[c] 364.00
Hungary	293.75	[d] 75.00	158.75	60.00	------	170.00	10.00	57.5–[e] 59.5
Mongolia	50.00	[f] 50.00	------	------	([g])	------	75.00	------
North Korea	42.50	------	------	------	42.50	------	141.00	------
North Viet-Nam	------	------	------	------	------	------	[h] 50.00	------
Poland	300.00	------	[i] 300.00	([i])	------	525.00	------	[j] 60.00
Rumania	103.50	67.50	[k] (36.00)	------	------	717.00	------	([l])
Total	1,260.00	300.00	677.90	240.00	42.50	1,517.50	226.00	------

[a] Only new officially acknowledged and publicly reported agreements have been included in this table.
[b] Communist China reported to have received loans of $58 million, but these probably were on account of earlier credit arrangements.
[c] Amount of annual reduction of East German contribution to maintenance of Soviet occupation troops.
[d] Also Hungarian uranium mining development credit of unspecified amount.
[e] Postponement of repayment of earlier credits to Hungary worth $37.5 million and $20–22 million readjustment of cost of Soviet noncommercial use of Hungarian transport.
[f] Additional development credits of unknown value.
[g] Mongolia must pay for Soviet properties transferred by the U.S.S.R.
[h] Aid deliveries in 1955–56.
i Poland also was to receive a small amount of gold of unknown value.
[j] Soviet payment for use of Polish rail transit facilities.
[k] Estimated value of grain credit.
[l] Repayment of unspecified credits postponed.

U.S.S.R. In 1956–57 about $1.5 billion in long-term credits and grants—mostly for early utilization—was extended by the U.S.S.R. to other members of the bloc (see Table 1, p. 16). In addition, the U.S.S.R. canceled debts worth more than $1.5 billion and made other forms of concessions, adjustments, and postponements. Although the U.S.S.R. claims to have given credits worth 21 billion rubles ($5.25 billion) prior to 1956, throughout most of the postwar period Soviet-satellite economic relations were marked by a high degree of Soviet exploitation of the satellite economies. Soviet economic assistance was for the most part sporadic, occasional, emergency in nature, and involved little drain on the Soviet economy. The economic aid granted to the satellites since 1956—and especially since the Hungarian revolt and the change of government in Poland in October 1956—has differed sufficiently in character as to constitute a new burden on the Soviet economy.

In addition to its credit program the Soviet Union must also provide much in the way of capital resources through trade channels to other bloc countries, especially China. Although still a net importer of machinery and equipment, even in its relations with the bloc, the U.S.S.R. claims in 1956 to have shipped machinery and equipment for 478 enterprises in other orbit countries.

The Cost of Foreign Aid

Despite the demands of the military effort, of domestic investment, of the neglected consumer sector, and of other bloc countries, the Soviet leadership has seen fit to impose the added burden of foreign aid commitments. Commitments incurred to date are substantial, although the annual burden is considerably less than the statistics might suggest inasmuch as deliveries are to be spread over a number of years. Several major Soviet credit agreements provide for drawings over periods as long as 5, 7, or even 8 years. Furthermore, as repayments on Soviet credits begin to increase, continuing aid of a given magnitude will represent a diminishing drain on overall resources. Soviet authorities will, of course, be faced with the necessity of making modifications in their internal economic plans in order to realize maximum economic benefits from such repayments.

Program Geared to Soviet Capabilities

Production in the U.S.S.R. is sufficiently great and variegated that a respectable variety of goods and services may be squeezed from the economy for export if political considerations require it. The U.S.S.R. attempts to minimize the domestic effects of its aid programs by utilizing goods and services in relatively less restricted supply to fulfill its foreign commitments. Because of unevenness in plan fulfillment and other causes, specific surpluses may develop and specific capacities may be underemployed—sometimes as a result of bottlenecks elsewhere in the economy.

Where a given project would have involved a significant drain on scarce Soviet resources, with the possible consequent threat to domestic industrial growth rates, the U.S.S.R. has rejected, stretched out, or postponed implementation. Examples include the aluminum complex in Yugoslavia and projects under the $126 million credit to India, which cannot be drawn upon until 1959. However, the "shopping lists" of the less developed countries contain such extensive and varied needs that the U.S.S.R. can provide many types of aid they urgently desire while still dovetailing the programs to Soviet domestic capabilities. In this way Soviet planners have been able to reduce the conflict between the claims of current domestic economic plans and those of foreign aid programs designed to further Soviet political objectives abroad.

A qualitative examination of the nature of U.S.S.R. commitments for aid and trade with the underdeveloped countries shows that, on the whole, the U.S.S.R. has thus far committed itself to a relatively limited range of machinery exports. These have included transportation, agricultural, and generating equipment. Road building and irrigation projects, hospitals, hydroelectric and irrigation dams, railroad and port construction, bakeries and silos, and laboratories have characterized Soviet projects to date. The U.S.S.R. is also stressing psychological showcase items such as nuclear research laboratories which have a broad popular appeal. Thus the U.S.S.R. in implementing its aid programs may choose to stress those projects which involve relatively heavier demands for Soviet engineers and technicians (who are available in substantial numbers) and equipment and materials which are in less short supply. Many Soviet projects also involve a relatively high proportion of local labor and materials.

Finally, the U.S.S.R. can virtually ignore domestic economic considerations in specific cases where it seems that the results would be sufficiently spectacular to justify such action. The Bhilai steel mill being built in India, which is unique in present Soviet programs, is an example of the U.S.S.R.'s readiness to divert scarce resources to its foreign aid programs even at the expense of some retardation of Soviet industrial growth.

Bloc Capabilities Expanded by Satellites' Contribution

In the field of industrial machinery and equipment, the U.S.S.R. can rely heavily on the export capabilities of its European satellites. Czechoslovakia and East Germany are traditional exporters of manufactured goods (including machinery and equipment) to the less developed countries in exchange for raw materials. The forced draft industrialization of the Stalinist period served to distort the economies of some of the European satellites, which now find themselves with top-heavy industrial capacities, marketing difficulties, and shortages of foods and raw materials. As a result, their economic motives for actively seeking trade with the less developed countries are stronger than ever. By contrast with the U.S.S.R., they have been active in offering these countries a wide range of capital goods, including complete industrial plants, both on regular commercial terms and on credit.[1] To the extent that such trade is

[1] Examples include: Czechoslovakia—ceramic factories, petroleum refineries, textile mills, sugar refineries, tanneries, shoe factories, machine shops, cement plants, a tire factory; East Germany—flour mills, textile plants, cement plants, sugar refineries, and aluminum complexes; Poland—sugar refineries, ships, railway equipment, plants to manufacture electrical machinery; Hungary—flour mills, communications equipment, railway equipment, power plants; Rumania—oil drilling equipment.

financed by credits, it represents a temporary burden. Moreover, the satellites have been aided in extending credits to the less developed countries by Soviet credits to the satellites.

That the U.S.S.R. can rely more heavily on the satellites in the economic offensive in the underdeveloped countries is seen by the recent amendment to the U.S.S.R.–Syrian aid agreement, which permits the utilization of U.S.S.R. credits for purchases in the satellite countries. Arrangements of this type will serve to relieve the pressure on scarce U.S.S.R. resources as well as to bolster satellite economies. Even in the trade field, a few of the more spectacular U.S.S.R. purchases of raw materials in the underdeveloped countries, e. g., Burma, were managed by a trilateral settlement involving Czechoslovak exports. Thus the satellite empire of the Soviet Union, while constituting a new burden on Soviet resources, can and does play a significant role in expanding bloc capabilities to wage the economic offensive.

In recent years even Communist China—despite its appalling internal problems—has actively entered the field of foreign aid. It has extended grants and credits to Ceylon, Nepal, Cambodia, Egypt, and Yemen. In the case of Ceylon the motivation was both political and economic; in the other cases, Communist Chinese assistance was extended almost entirely for political reasons. With large import requirements for its rapidly increasing industries, small though they still are, Communist China has to boost its foreign exchange availabilities, and it considers some credits, within the limits of its modest capabilities, a key to open new markets. Communist China's exports to the free world ran from $300 million in 1954 to $540 million in 1956 and a probably similar amount in 1957. Of total Communist Chinese trade turnover—planned at $4.2 billion in 1957—about 75 percent is with the Soviet bloc, and there is little likelihood of a significant change in this regard in the near future.

Capability of Furnishing Arms

With regard to arms deals—either on commercial terms or credit—both the U.S.S.R. and the satellites have the capacity to expand past operations substantially. While some of the military items provided include late model equipment, a considerable part has been obsolescent by Soviet military standards. These deals—even at comparatively low prices—did not impose substantial costs and may even have produced a net economic gain.

Capability of Furnishing Technicians

It is not possible to estimate precisely the number of technicians that could be sent abroad by the bloc countries. However, the bloc is capable of a substantial increase in its current technical assistance effort in view of the existing pool of trained manpower in the U.S.S.R. and the technical training currently taking place. Moreover, in an authoritarian state the assignment of personnel to support foreign programs involves relatively few recruitment problems.

In the U.S.S.R., official figures show that at the end of 1956, 720,900 engineers; 179,500 agronomists, veterinarians, and foresters; and 130,200 economists, statisticians, and commodity experts were employed in nonteaching jobs. To this group of 1,020,600 trained in higher educational institutions may be added 1,550,000 persons with secondary education in the same categories. Plans for 1956–60 indicate that the number of "specialists" with secondary or higher education in industry, agriculture, construction, and transportation will increase by an amount double the number trained in 1951–55, which could raise the total number employed by 30–50 percent. In some key categories the Soviet pool of specialists exceeds that of the United States and is growing at a much faster rate.

Capabilities Stemming From the System

Centralized economic planning and control, as well as the state trading monopolies that characterize the Communist system, facilitate the manipulation of foreign trade and aid programs. Decisions can be made on the diversion of resources from domestic to foreign assistance programs without legislative authorization. Decisions as to pricing and choices of products to be imported and exported can be made with respect to opportunities for political gain, with economic considerations relegated to second place. These factors combine to create the impression in the less developed countries that bloc programs have great flexibility and are conducted efficiently and expeditiously.

In the context of capabilities, it may be significant that, although Soviet domestic mass media have discussed the problem of "economic collaboration" with the underdeveloped countries, they have carefully avoided informing the Soviet people of the magnitude of total Soviet aid commitments. Moreover, while the Soviet publications have in a sense appealed to the pride of the population by accounts of some of the assistance rendered to key countries, they have toned down considerably for domestic consumption the accounts of the more sweeping and dramatic aid offers made abroad.

Bloc Capabilities and Future Prospects

To sum up, capabilities are relative to the size and character of the job to be done. The U.S.S.R. is the second greatest economic power in the world, and its capabilities in the economic field, despite recent signs of difficulty, are still growing at a rapid rate. Moreover, its capabilities are considerably abetted by the industrialized European satellites. The total bloc aid program can, therefore, be expanded considerably and extended to still more countries. Recent Soviet overtures suggest that the U.S.S.R. contemplates such expansion by extending credits to other countries rather than by substantially increasing commitments to countries which are already major recipients. Because of the nature of the U.S.S.R.'s political objectives, discussed in Chapter II, its programs do not require the substantial sums that would be necessary if the bloc were seriously concerned with promoting balanced, long-term economic growth in the less developed countries. Above all, the Soviet leaders have in the past clearly demonstrated their willingness to incur substantial economic costs to gain specific political objectives.

IV. THE NATURE OF THE OFFENSIVE

Assistance Programs

Magnitude and Recipients. Since 1954 the Soviet-bloc countries have concluded agreements with 14 of the less developed countries outside the Soviet orbit which provide for the extension of an estimated $1.9 billion in intermediate and long-term credits for the purchase of goods and services from the bloc. Of this total, about $378 million consisted of credits for the purchase of Soviet-bloc arms extended to Egypt, Syria, Yemen, and Afghanistan. The remaining $1.5 billion for economic purposes includes $464 million in credits to Yugoslavia, which, as a Communist country, represents a special case. Communist China is the only bloc country providing grants of any consequence. To date it has granted $55 million to Cambodia, Ceylon, Nepal, and Egypt (see Table 2, p. 23).

The U.S.S.R is providing about $1.3 billion of the total credits; the remaining $600 million is almost entirely accounted for by the satellites. Some of the major arms deals entered into by the latter quite obviously involved Soviet participation. As regards development credits, the U.S.S.R. has concentrated its activities in a relatively few major deals: $100 million credit agreements with Afghanistan and Indonesia; $132 million for a steel mill and another $126 million credit for India; a $110 million credit for Yugoslavia and $175 million (jointly with East Germany) for an aluminum complex; agreements of $175 million for Egypt and an estimated $168 million for Syria. The many nonmilitary credits granted by the satellites have involved, as a rule, amounts of only a few million dollars each.

The bloc maximizes the political and psychological impact of its program by concentrating its aid in a few key countries where situations exist that lend themselves to exploitation for the attainment of bloc objectives. Yugoslavia, India, Afghanistan, Egypt, Syria, and Indonesia have received more than 95 percent of the credits.[1] Iran, Turkey, and Iceland are notable examples of countries allied with the West which have been the targets of continuing bloc offers; all have accepted limited economic aid.

Utilization. The drawings under these credits will be spread over several years; in the case of the recent Syrian credit, for example, the program will extend over 7 years. As of December 31, 1957, an estimated two-thirds of bloc credits had been earmarked for specific projects or were under firm contract. However, only about 30 percent of the credits had actually been drawn, including most of the arms credits but only 10–15 percent of the economic credits.

---

[1] The remainder is accounted for by Turkey, Yemen, Burma, Ceylon, Iceland, Argentina, and Brazil.

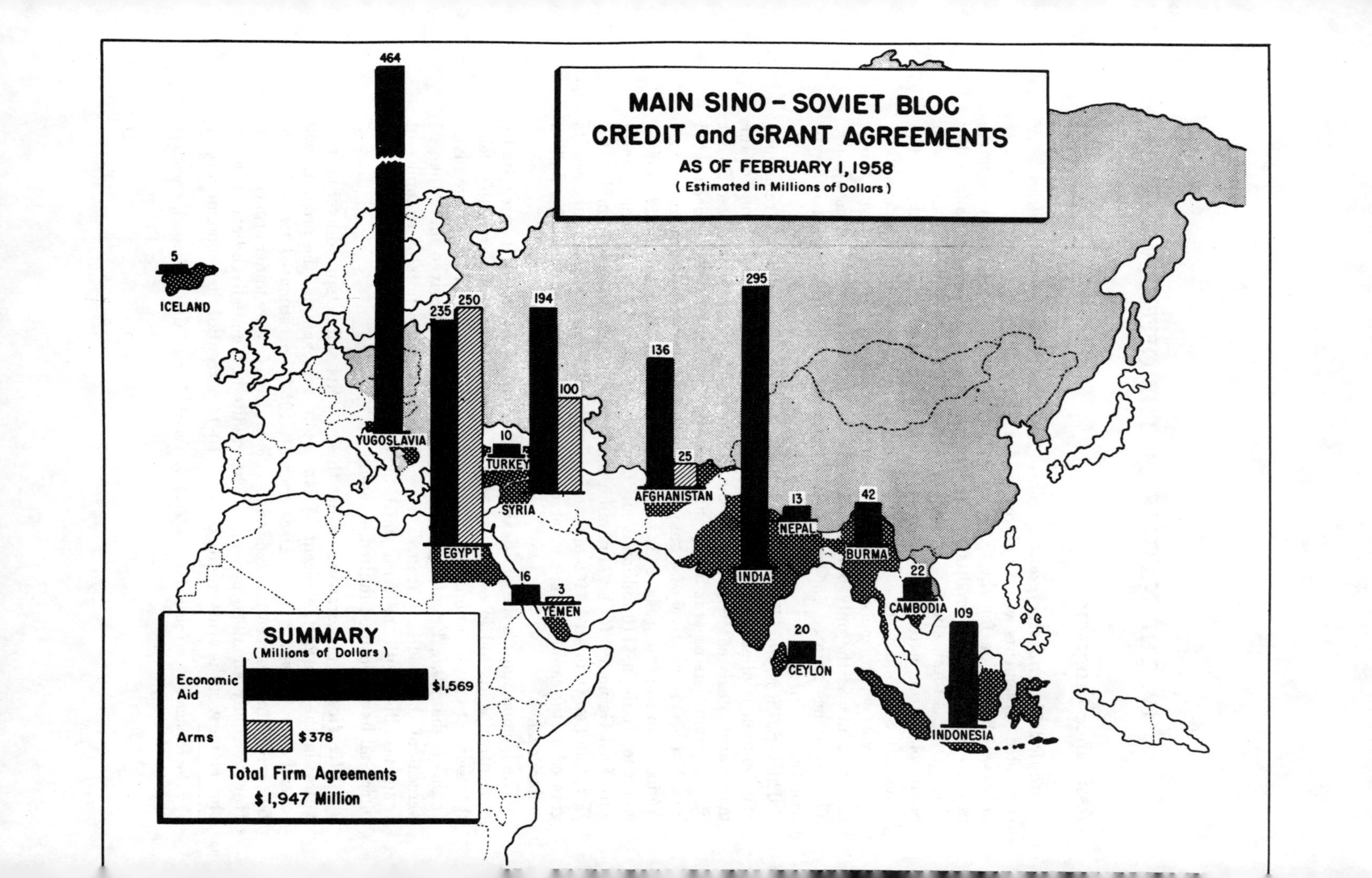
MAIN SINO - SOVIET BLOC
CREDIT and GRANT AGREEMENTS
AS OF FEBRUARY 1, 1958
(Estimated in Millions of Dollars)
5
ICELAND
464
YUGOSLAVIA
235
250
EGYPT
10
TURKEY
194
100
SYRIA
16
3
YEMEN
136
25
AFGHANISTAN
295
INDIA
13
NEPAL
42
BURMA
20
CEYLON
22
CAMBODIA
109
INDONESIA
SUMMARY
(Millions of Dollars)
Economic Aid
$1,569
Arms
$378
Total Firm Agreements
$1,947 Million

Table 2. *Estimated Sino-Soviet Bloc Credits and Grants* [a] *to Less Developed Countries Through February 1, 1958*

(Millions of U.S. dollar equivalents)

Country	Total	Economic	Military
Grand Total	1,947	1,569	378
Near East and Africa	808	455	353
Egypt	485	235	250
Syria	294	194	100
Turkey	10	10	------
Yemen	19	16	3
South and Southeast Asia	662	637	25
Afghanistan	161	136	25
Burma	42	42	------
Cambodia	22	22	------
Ceylon	20	20	------
India	295	295	------
Indonesia	109	109	------
Nepal	13	13	------
Europe	469	469	0
Iceland	5	5	------
Yugoslavia	464	464	------
Latin America	8	8	0

[a] Credits except for Communist Chinese grants of $22 million to Cambodia, $13 million to Nepal, $16 million to Ceylon, and $5 million to Egypt. Burma is receiving several "gift" projects from the U.S.S.R. but will make a return gift of rice to the U.S.S.R. over an extended period.

While a substantial amount of the required planning and survey work for projects is completed or well advanced, the major construction work actually under way so far on Soviet projects is in India and Afghanistan. A number of smaller satellite projects have been started.

Credits Rather Than Grants. Virtually all Soviet and satellite assistance is in the form of interest-bearing credits to finance specific development projects. The Soviets probably wish to give the impression of making businesslike deals, feeling that interest-free loans or grants arouse suspicion as to "strings" in the recipient countries. Obviously the prospect of repayment with interest, even if at a low rate, makes the assistance less costly to the U.S.S.R. Although economic return is a secondary consideration, the impression conveyed by the interest rate to public opinion within the bloc is that Soviet foreign assistance is "mutually profitable" and that the only reason the West charges higher rates is to reap "capitalist profits." The use of credits rather than grants also serves as a restraint on the volume of requests, enabling the U.S.S.R. from the outset to limit the overall scope of its aid program with minimally adverse political effects. Finally, since the use of credits implies that throughout the repayment period some of the exports of the debtors will be diverted away from the traditional markets in the West, the Soviets will be able to maintain continuing relations with the target countries.

Interest Rates. One of the features of Soviet credits to less developed countries which has attracted great attention has been the low interest rates, typically 2.5 percent. There is little information available on the terms of credit extended by the satellites, but a few of these have carried somewhat higher rates. The interest rate on Soviet credits is presumably motivated politically rather than based on economic calculations. These rates approximate the Soviet State Bank's domestic interest rates on short-term loans although the foreign credits are long term and for investment purposes. Soviet theory and practice do not even recognize the use of interest charges internally on investment capital. The chronically severe shortage of capital in the U.S.S.R. in relation to planned investment would undoubtedly impose a considerably higher rate than is used in Soviet foreign credits.

Interest rates on Soviet loans to less developed countries probably bear some relation to the rates charged on Soviet loans to the satellite countries, which are generally 2 percent and in several instances, e. g., the 1950 loan to Communist China, as low as 1 percent. These rates apparently provide the floor, while Western rates for comparable purposes impose a ceiling, which is approached only in the case of credits advanced by the satellites to the less developed countries. The U.S.S.R.'s interest charge of 2.5 percent to the less developed countries preserves the preferential status of the satellites, since as members of the "Socialist camp" they receive a rate which is lower, and at the same time satisfies the less developed borrowers, who are charged only one half of 1 percent more than members of the bloc.

Prices and Value. Major Soviet credit agreements have been expressed in terms of rubles, dollars, or local currencies of fixed gold content. The choice of currency is, in fact, immaterial to a calculation of the value to be received. The recent use in Soviet agreements with India, Syria, and Egypt of rubles of fixed gold content (i. e., at the official rate of 4 rubles to the dollar) is significant only from the point of view of Soviet prestige considerations.

Both foreign trade and foreign assistance programs are planned by the U.S.S.R. in physical terms and are carried on by state trade organizations with foreign countries in terms of world market prices, which are not correlated with Soviet domestic prices. In fact, one of the basic purposes of foreign trade monopolies in the Soviet bloc is to insulate the bloc domestic price systems from "capitalist" prices, i. e., the world market. These systems are manipulated to support domestic economic programs in the U.S.S.R. and other bloc countries.

The limited evidence available suggests that the Soviet bloc in general uses world market prices as a yardstick for its own prices in contracts with underdeveloped countries. In a few instances bloc countries have underbid the West on contracts that they were particularly eager to obtain. Where there have been occasional complaints that bloc bids were too high, the excessive prices asked may have stemmed from the difficulty of formulating bids on a unique and complex development project when no prior Western competition afforded a standard. In several such cases, the bloc bid has subsequently been reduced.

On the other hand, certain Soviet prices have been considered too high by some countries, such as Afghanistan. In some instances, the U.S.S.R. may quote high prices as a device to discourage foreign demands for specific goods it does not want to supply.

Repayment Terms. Many of the major Soviet credit agreements provide for annual negotiations in the future to establish lists, prices, and quantities of goods to be delivered in repayment, as well as the proportion of goods and convertible currency for each annual installment (see Table 3, p. 26). In view of the limited experience in regard to repayment of Soviet credits, it is not clear just what these provisions imply. They obviously leave a large area for later bargaining, which may become a source of friction, although the U.S.S.R. may also use the negotiations as an opportunity for politically motivated "generosity." The provision for annual agreements on goods accepted in repayment would seem designed, at a minimum, to protect the U.S.S.R. against local price rises not reflected in world price levels, and against having to accept goods unwanted or in unwanted quantities. By deferring to later bargaining the proportions of goods and convertible currency in the annual repayment, the U.S.S.R. will be in a position to demand a major portion in convertible currency if price rises make repayment in goods less attractive. Such a demand would be subject, of course, to the agreement of the debtor country, which might be caught, however, between acceptance of unfavorable prices and relinquishment of scarce foreign exchange. If the recipient country wants no more Soviet aid, its bargaining position is likely to be stronger. In this regard, the language of certain agreements is susceptible to an interpretation which would give the U.S.S.R. a unilateral option between goods and convertible currency; if this is the case, the U.S.S.R. would appear to be well protected against losses from price increases and by the same token to have a potent bargaining lever.

In its most recent deals, the U.S.S.R. has agreed to defer the beginning of the repayment process for any given project until completion of all deliveries. For the recipients of assistance this is attractive because it permits production to begin before payments are due.

Aside from political considerations, involving, for example, the playing off of alternative sources of supply against one another, the U.S.S.R.'s willingness to accept particular commodities from a debtor country in repayment is affected by its domestic supply situation. Although the U.S.S.R.'s economy continues to be plagued by scarcities, its willingness to accept commodities in repayment may vary considerably in accordance with the commodity in question. Some of the exports of the underdeveloped countries are of great importance to the Soviet economy (e. g., Indonesian and Ceylonese rubber), and the U.S.S.R. may even be willing to accept these commodities at higher prices that those of the world market in repayment for its credits. Other products can be absorbed but are of secondary importance to the Soviet economy from the planners' point of view (e. g., rice, cocoa, tea, coffee, raisins, and spices). Still others may not be easily absorbed either because the Soviet economy lacks sufficient processing capacity or has sufficient domestic supplies. Soviet programs to increase production at home of cotton, wheat, wool, and hides, for example, may limit, though they obviously do not exclude, imports of these products from Egypt, Syria, and Afghanistan.

TABLE 3. *Terms of Selected Major Credit Agreements of the Bloc*

Country, amount, and interest rate	Period	Means of repayment	Other repayment provisions
India–U.S.S.R. Feb. 8, 1955 $132.2 million (Bhilai steel mill) 2.5 percent interest	First payment due 1 year after each consignment; 12 annual payments	Rupees of present gold content	Utilizable "for purchase of goods and/or freely convertible into pounds sterling"; Reserve Bank of India and Gosbank will jointly fix technical procedure of settling this account.
Afghanistan–U.S.S.R. Jan. 28, 1956 $100 million 2.0 percent interest	First payment due in 8 years; 22 annual payments	"Afghan export goods"	Arrangements to be made by Gosbank and State Bank of Afghanistan
Indonesia–U.S.S.R. Sept. 15, 1956 $100 million 2.5 percent interest	First payment due 3 years after each fractional credit; 12 annual payments	Goods or sterling or convertible foreign exchange at rate of exchange of the dollar on date of repayment	On the basis of an advance agreement between Gosbank and Bank of Indonesia, "list of the goods to be delivered and quantity, price and time of delivery" determined by both sides 3 months before year of each payment
India–U.S.S.R. Nov. 15, 1956; implementation agreement Nov. 13, 1957 $126 million 2.5 percent interest	First payment due 1 year after entire enterprise; 12 annual installments	Rupees (presumably as Feb. 8, 1955, credit)	
Syria–U.S.S.R. Oct. 28, 1957 Estimated $168 million 2.5 percent interest	(as amended) First payment due 1 year after project completed; 12 annual payments	Goods or freely convertible currency at rate of exchange of ruble on date of repayment	In accordance with an agreement to be concluded between Syrian Central Bank and Gosbank; lists of goods, quantity, prices, and time of delivery settled 3 months before each year of payment.

TABLE 3. *Terms of Selected Major Credit Agreements of the Bloc*—Continued

Country, amount, and interest rate	Period	Means of repayment	Other repayment provisions
Egypt–U.S.S.R. Jan. 29, 1958 $175 million 2.5 percent interest	12 annual payments after project completed	(Presumably similar to Syrian)	
Syria–Czechoslovakia. Mar. 16, 1957 $15 million (oil refinery) 3.0 percent interest	60 percent at specified times during construction; 40 percent in 7 years afterwards	23 percent Syrian lira; 77 percent sterling	

When the U.S.S.R. takes commodities of secondary importance to its economy or redundant to its needs at any given time, there is the possibility that it will resell these on the world market for convertible currencies. This may have occurred in the case of Egyptian cotton, Burmese rice, and Syrian wheat.

Administration of Aid Programs. Dramatic and well publicized visits and conferences of high-level officials have been used by the bloc to promote the economic offensive. In a number of cases, especially those involving the U.S.S.R., agreements in principle to provide assistance have been made by high ministerial and party officials in a blaze of publicity calculated to reap maximum propaganda advantage. These have been quickly followed up by the negotiation of general assistance agreements which ordinarily specify a total amount of credit and terms. They are either accompanied or quite rapidly followed up by the negotiation of further agreements which settle the types of projects to be undertaken. Thereafter, technical surveys are initiated and specific contracts signed. Since propaganda accompanies each stage, a multiple publicity effect is achieved.

The secrecy of policy decisions under the totalitarian system characterizes bloc aid programs. Public or legislative debate, which would air such subjects as Soviet motives or the situation in recipient countries, is unthinkable in the U.S.S.R. This is quite the reverse of the procedure in democratic countries, where foreign aid proposals are subjected to close and detailed public scrutiny.

In the U.S.S.R. the foreign assistance program is administered by the State Committee for External Economic Relations of the Soviet Council of Ministers. The establishment of this State Committee in July 1957 represents an upgrading of the assistance programs in the Soviet bureaucratic hierarchy. Most of the general agreements are negotiated by one of the four deputy chairmen of the State Committee; the composition of the Soviet delegations indicates that the State Committee coordinates the activities of other ministries in the foreign assistance program.

The State Committee is organized on both a geographical and functional basis. The existence of a Treaty-Legal Section and a Protocol Section indicates the importance and scope of its operations. Among the functional divisions are an Administration for Construction of Enterprises Abroad, a Section for Industry and Transport, a Section for Agriculture, a Section for Finances and Internal Trade, a Main Engineering Administration (probably the organization administering military assistance), and an Administration for Matters of Scientific-Technical Cooperation.

On a geographic basis, there are Sections for Europe, the "East," and "Underdeveloped Capitalist Countries." There are also Commissions for Scientific-Technical Cooperation for all the Sino-Soviet bloc countries except North Viet-Nam and Mongolia, plus Yugoslavia and Finland. Several foreign trade organizations which specialize in development projects have been transferred to the Committee from the Ministry of Foreign Trade. These organizations survey the actual projects, negotiate the contracts, and carry out the work.

While the activities of the satellites in the field of foreign economic aid are not on the scale of those of the U.S.S.R., they are of sufficient importance to require some coordinating machinery. In some of the satellites the Foreign Trade Ministries are the coordinating agencies of the foreign assistance programs. To date there is no official institutional framework for the bloc-wide coordination of the economic offensive. In some cases, notably the Czechoslovak arms credits to Egypt, such coordination was obvious. However, there have been cases in which bloc countries have competed against each other for specific projects.

The bloc generally implements its aid programs on a project basis without establishing an overall, centralized organization within the recipient country. The Soviet Embassy apparently serves as the point of contact for the technicians. Delegation of authority gives the appearance of flexibility, although the survey data on proposed projects must be referred back to Moscow for the drawing up of the blueprints. Use is also made in some instances of mixed commissions of representatives and technicians from each country concerned with implementing aid agreements and supervising operations.

Most aid provided by the bloc is earmarked for specific projects, and the necessary officials and technicians are sent to do particular jobs, after which they return home, except for a few who may remain to supervise operations. Bloc personnel, therefore, do not ordinarily get involved in follow-up problems.

Finally, in some countries (e. g., India) the U.S.S.R. is careful not to assume responsibility for organizing or managing the project. The Bhilai steel mill, for example, is an Indian project with Soviet specialists acting in staff capacities, and no Indian works for a Russian on that project. It is believed the U.S.S.R. will try to follow this pattern wherever practical, notably in such countries as Egypt and Syria. The aid agreement with Syria specifically states that Syria will organize all work related to the project. By such procedures, the U.S.S.R. doubtless hopes to minimize frictions in the recipient countries and particularly to avoid the appearance of foreign "domination." Moreover, any subsequent difficulties which arise can less easily be blamed on the bloc.

Military Assistance. Of the $378 million in bloc military credits, the bulk has gone to Egypt and Syria. For the most part such aid has already been delivered. Credits have been provided for training and arms, including the construction of airfields and naval installations in some cases. Military

A Soviet technician from Turkistan (left) at the site of a grain silo under construction by the U.S.S.R. at Pul-i-Khumri, Afghanistan.

assistance has been made available to four countries, all of which are involved in political difficulties with their neighbors. This military aid serves the purpose of increasing tensions in order to create a more receptive climate for the extension of Soviet influence. In its shipments of arms, the bloc does not require any commitment that the arms will be used only for defensive purposes.

Technical Assistance. Technical assistance provided by the bloc is closely related to its trade and credit activities and is not a separate program on a grant basis as is that of the United States. Over 2,300 bloc technicians spent a month or more in 19 less developed countries during the last half of 1957, while another 2,000 technicians and students from the less developed countries have gone to the bloc for study and training during the past year. Of these, 500 have enrolled in universities or for other advanced training.

Nearly 1,600 of the bloc technicians sent abroad were involved in economic development work (see Table 4, p. 30). All are paid for by the recipient government, but the majority are engaged on projects being partially financed by bloc credits. Bloc military specialists engaged in assembling bloc equipment and training local forces numbered about 800. Like bloc credits, technical assistance is highly concentrated. About 80 percent of all bloc technicians are found in Egypt, Syria, India, Indonesia, and Afghanistan. In general, the bloc has endeavored to select technicians appearing competent in their field of specialization. Language difficulties have created some problems, and the extent of contacts with the local populations varies from project to project. While bloc technicians have, on the whole, been careful to avoid the appearance of engaging in overt propaganda or subversive activities, which are the responsibility of other bloc personnel, this type of assistance as well as training programs in the bloc provide a valuable means for influencing the nationals of the less developed countries, especially the increasingly influential groups of scientists, technicians, and government administrators, in directions favorable to Communists.

Character of Bloc Aid Programs. There are serious disadvantages to Soviet aid for recipient countries as compared with Western credits. In utilizing Soviet credits for development purposes, the recipient is narrowly confined in choosing the goods and services that will be supplied. Even a "tied" loan from a Western country permits the recipient to shop in a market

TABLE 4. *Sino-Soviet Bloc Industrial, Agricultural, and Other Professional Specialists in Less Developed Countries* [a]

July–December 1957

Area and country	Total bloc
Total	1, 585
NEAR EAST AND AFRICA	565
Egypt	360
Greece	10
Iran	5
Sudan	10
Syria	110
Turkey	15
Yemen	55
SOUTH AND SOUTHEAST ASIA	915
Afghanistan	455
Burma	60
Cambodia	30
Ceylon	5
India	260
Indonesia	105
LATIN AMERICA	55
Argentina	50
Bolivia	([b])
Brazil	([b])
Chile	([b])
Mexico	([b])
EUROPE	
Yugoslavia	50

[a] Minimum estimates of personnel working on a contract basis for a period of 1 month or more. Personnel solely in trade promotion or military activities are excluded. Because of rounding, figures do not necessarily add to the totals shown. Numbers are rounded to the nearest five.

[b] One or two bloc specialists believed to be present.

composed of many private suppliers and to pick and choose from among a wide assortment of goods and services. Thus bloc credits result in binding important development projects to limited bloc sources of supply, with further disadvantages (discussed under the heading of The Trade Drive, below) looming as possibilities. For example, diversion of a country's exports to the bloc in order to repay the credits acts to deprive that country of its traditional free-world markets.

The psychological impact of the bloc aid program in recipient countries is due in large part to its novelty. This feature will, of course, diminish with the passing of time, and as recipient countries have the opportunity to appraise the real value of aid deals with the bloc. While bloc programs involve a variety of projects, an attempt has been made to emphasize those which will have great psychological effect. In particular, deals which have some manufacturing component lend credence in the less developed countries to bloc propaganda claims that its programs are aimed at achievement of rapid industrialization. Given the political nature of the bloc offensive, the propaganda reward is an important aspect.

The Trade Drive

Prior to 1953 the Soviet Union showed little interest in developing trade with the less developed countries. While the U.S.S.R., as a matter of policy, has always tried to maintain an overall balance in its imports and exports, the less developed countries were viewed largely as an occasional source of various types of raw materials not available within the Soviet orbit; for the most part the U.S.S.R. paid for these purchases by proceeds of sales to the industrialized nations of the West. Increasingly since 1953, trade offers—both on the export and import sides—have played a growing role in Soviet attempts to gain increased political influence. The U.S.S.R. and other bloc countries have stepped up both the tempo and scope of their trade promotion drive—sending out a large number of trade missions, pressing the conclusion of bilateral trade agreements, participating extensively in trade fairs and exhibitions, and stressing opportunities for expanded trade in their propaganda media. Although the foreign aid side of the economic offensive has received the most publicity in the free world, the Soviet's own statements have emphasized the trade aspect. For example, a leading Soviet economist has stated, "The most important form of economic cooperation of the U.S.S.R. with other powers, including the countries which are poorly developed in regard to economic relationships, is foreign trade. . . ." [2]

Value and Pattern of Trade. Total trade turnover of the bloc with less developed countries increased from $850 million in 1954 to $1.44 billion in 1956, or about 70 percent. Partial data for 1957 suggest that bloc trade with less developed countries probably rose by 20–25 percent over 1956, i. e., to at least double the level of 1954. Because Soviet and Communist Chinese exports have risen substantially more than imports from these countries, the trade

[2] Alkhimov, V., "Cooperation between the U.S.S.R. and Economically Underdeveloped Countries," *Voprosi Ekonomiki*, No. 6, June 1957.

deficit characteristic of earlier periods was converted to a surplus in 1956. A near balancing of trade probably occurred in 1957.

From 1954 through 1956, Soviet trade with these countries rose by $174 million, satellite trade by $294 million, and Communist Chinese trade by $126 million. Of total bloc trade with the free world, that with the less developed countries amounts to 27.5 percent in 1956. The trade of the individual bloc countries with the less developed countries is still a relatively small proportion of the former's total trade (including trade with bloc partners), but represents a considerably larger share of their trade with the free world. For example, in 1956 trade with the less developed area represented about 5 to 6 percent of Soviet total foreign trade but about 25 percent of Soviet trade with the free world. In the case of Communist China, trade with the area accounted for about 7 percent of total trade but 30 percent of trade with the free world. There are wide variations in the corresponding ratios in the European satellites, the highest percentages being attained in the case of Czechoslovakia—13 percent of total trade and 46 percent of trade with the free world (see table below).

In 1956 the European satellites accounted for about half of bloc trade with these areas (Czechoslovakia, 23 percent; the U.S.S.R., 26 percent; and Communist China, 22 percent). In 1957 the U.S.S.R. probably accounted for a somewhat larger share of the total due mainly to substantial purchases of a few raw materials. Nevertheless, the European satellites have been and will probably continue to provide the main force for the trade offensive.

TABLE 5. *The Geographical Pattern of Sino-Soviet Bloc Trade, 1956* [a]

(In millions of U. S. dollars)

	U.S.S.R.	Communist China	East Germany	Czechoslovakia	Poland	Rumania	Hungary	Bulgaria
Total	7, 280	4, 415	2, 750	2, 600	1, 876	(925)	950	515
Bloc	5, 405	3, 325	2, 005	1, 675	1, 134	(740)	590	440
Percent	74. 2	75. 3	73. 0	64. 5	60. 2	80. 0	62. 1	85. 5
U.S.S.R.	------	2, 370	(1, 125)	(825)	513	445	226	(245)
Percent	------	53. 7	41. 0	31. 8	27. 5	47. 6	23. 8	(47. 6)
European satellites	3, 585	760	(760)	(710)	540	(280)	290	(195)
Percent	48. 8	17. 2	(27. 6)	(27. 3)	(28. 8)	(30. 3)	(30. 5)	(37. 9)
Communist China	1, 497	------	120	n.a.	80	n.a.	60	n.a.
Percent	20. 5	------	80. 0	------	4. 5	------	6. 2	------
Free world	1, 875	1, 090	735	925	726	(185)	360	75
Percent	25. 8	24. 7	27. 0	35. 5	39. 8	20. 0	37. 9	14. 5
Free world [b]	1, 585	1, 054	663	735	797	187	314	75
Less developed countries [b]	400	330	87	338	156	60	94	21
Less developed countries As percent of free world	25. 2	30. 3	8. 3	46. 0	19. 6	32. 0	29. 9	28. 0
Less developed countries As percent of total trade	5. 5	7. 5	3. 2	13. 0	8. 3	6. 5	9. 9	4. 1

[a] Statistics are from official statistics and statements of respective countries; figures in parenthesis are estimates.
[b] Statistics from U. S. Department of Commerce.
n. a.—not available.

While bloc trade promotion efforts have been widespread geographically, the major increases in actual trade with the less developed countries through 1956 were concentrated in a relatively few countries (see Tables 6 and 7, pp. 34 and 36). In fact, increased trade with five countries, Iceland, Egypt, India, Burma, and Yugoslavia, accounts for 82 percent of the increase in the bloc's trade between 1954 and 1956; 71 percent of the increase in exports, and 98 percent of the increase in imports. The magnitude of the latter figure is attributable in part to the fact that increases in bloc imports from these five countries coincided with a substantial decline in its imports from others among the less developed countries, notably Argentina, Uruguay, and to a lesser extent Ceylon.

An important share of the bloc's increase in trade with the less developed countries results from the rapid expansion of commerce with Yugoslavia following the political *rapprochement* in 1954. For example, $104.5 million of the $366.5 million increase in bloc exports to these countries in the 1954–56 period and $71.1 million of the $228 million increase in bloc imports is accounted for by Yugoslavia.

In addition to Iceland two other NATO countries, Greece and Turkey, had substantial increases in trade with the bloc between 1954 and 1956. Bloc trade with Indonesia and Malaya also showed a rapid rise in this period. Bloc trade with Syria showed a sharp percentage increase between 1954 and 1956 but still represented a minor part of Syria's total trade in the latter year. Preliminary information for 1957 indicates, however, that the bloc substantially increased its share of Syria's exports although the expansion of Syrian imports from the bloc was less marked.

There are wide variations in the percentage of the foreign trade of individual underdeveloped countries accounted for by the bloc. In 1956 exports to the bloc accounted for 10 percent or more of the total exports of Iceland, Yugoslavia, Egypt, Greece, Iran, Turkey, Burma, and Ceylon. Imports from the bloc were 10 percent or more of the total in the case of Iceland, Yugoslavia, Egypt, Turkey, and Burma (see Tables 8 and 9, pp. 37 and 38). While precise data are not available for Afghanistan, the U.S.S.R. alone claims to account for 35 percent of that country's foreign trade.

Commodity Composition of Bloc Trade. The U.S.S.R.'s exports to the less developed countries of the Middle East, South Asia, and Southeast Asia, according to Soviet statistics, consist primarily of rolled steel, petroleum and petroleum products, lumber, cement, cotton cloth, sugar, and wheat. The U.S.S.R. claims to have exported only $21.4 million worth of machinery and equipment (consisting to a large extent of automotive vehicles). Although five times greater than in 1955, these exports still did not constitute a very significant fulfillment of the propaganda claim of supplying the "means of production." This amount may have increased somewhat in 1957 and will probably become more significant when Soviet economic assistance credits are implemented. In more specific terms, however, the U.S.S.R. claims in 1956 to have accounted for 15 percent of Indian imports of rolled steel; 75 percent of Afghanistan's imports of petroleum products, 95 percent of its imports of sugar, 70 percent of its imports of cotton textiles, and 40 percent of its imports of automotive vehicles; 26 percent of Egypt's imports of petroleum, 42 percent of its imports of petroleum products, and 38 percent of its imports of wheat.

On the Soviet import side, the most important commodities received from these countries in 1956 were cotton, wool, raw hides, rubber, nonferrous metal ores, oilseeds, rice, tea, coffee, raisins, and spices. The U.S.S.R. claims to be the largest importer of Indian, Afghan, and Iranian raw hides; Egyptian cotton and rice; and Turkish cattle. It has purchased substantial amounts of Burmese rice, Moroccan citrus fruits, Indian spices, Afghan and Iranian cotton, wool, dried fruits, and oilseeds. In 1956 the U.S.S.R. obtained from the Middle East, South Asia, and Southeast Asia 100 percent of its imports of raw hides, jute bagging, and shellac, 97 percent of its imports of cotton, 74 percent of its imports of raisins, 37 percent of its imports of spices, 28 percent of its imports of rice, 20 percent of its imports of wool, citrus products, and tea. In addition, the U.S.S.R. buys significant quantities of sugar, cocoa, and rubber (including indirect purchases made in European countries).

TABLE 6. *Sino-Soviet Bloc Imports From Selected Less Developed Countries by Area and Country* [a]

1954–56

(Millions of U.S. dollars)

Area and country	U.S.S.R.			European satellites			Communist China			Total Sino-Soviet bloc		
	1954	1955	1956	1954	1955	1956	1954	1955	1956	1954	1955	1956
EUROPE												
Iceland	7.9	9.6	12.5	5.0	4.9	6.5	0.0	0.0	0.0	12.9	14.5	19.0
Spain	0.0	0.0	0.0	0.4	0.1	0.0	(b)	(b)	(b)	0.4	0.1	(b)
Yugoslavia	1.5	17.9	41.6	4.7	17.6	31.3	0.0	0.0	4.4	6.2	35.5	77.3
Subtotal	9.4	27.5	54.1	10.1	22.6	37.8	0.0	0.0	4.4	19.5	50.1	96.3
NEAR EAST AND AFRICA												
Egypt	5.4	20.2	16.0	39.5	61.4	99.0	11.4	24.5	24.2	56.3	106.1	139.2
Ghana	20.3	11.4	5.7	0.0	0.0	0.0	0.0	0.0	0.0	20.4	11.4	5.7
Greece	3.7	2.2	6.8	7.1	6.3	12.7	0.0	0.0	0.2	10.8	8.5	19.7
Iran	18.6	17.1	14.9	1.7	3.6	3.4	0.0	0.0	0.0	20.3	20.7	18.3
Iraq	0.1	0.0	0.0	0.0	0.1	0.0	0.0	0.0	0.0	0.1	0.1	0.0
Israel	3.1	1.7	1.6	1.3	1.7	3.1	0.0	0.0	0.0	4.4	3.4	4.7
Jordan	0.0	0.0	0.0	0.0	0.0	0.8	0.0	0.0	0.0	0.0	0.0	0.8
Lebanon	(b)	1.0	0.7	0.7	1.0	0.4	0.0	0.0	0.0	0.7	2.0	1.1
Morocco	0.6	1.7	0.2	2.3	7.7	4.5	0.0	0.0	0.0	2.9	9.4	4.7
Sudan	0.0	0.0	0.0	0.7	3.2	3.6	0.2	0.8	2.5	0.9	4.0	6.1
Syria	(b)	0.0	1.1	0.1	1.5	8.5	0.6	0.2	1.6	0.7	1.7	11.2
Turkey	5.2	5.2	6.6	50.0	63.4	53.4	0.0	0.0	(b)	55.1	68.6	60.0
Subtotal	57.0	60.5	53.6	103.4	149.9	189.4	12.2	25.5	28.5	172.6	235.9	271.5

TABLE 6. *Sino-Soviet Bloc Imports From Selected Less Developed Countries by Area and Country* [a]—Continued

1954–56

(Millions of U.S. dollars)

Area and country	U.S.S.R.			European satellites			Communist China			Total Sino-Soviet bloc		
	1954	1955	1956	1954	1955	1956	1954	1955	1956	1954	1955	1956
SOUTH AND SOUTHEAST ASIA												
Burma	0. 0	15. 2	11. 4	0. 0	10. 5	8. 9	0. 1	17. 5	14. 4	0. 1	43. 2	34. 7
Ceylon	0. 0	0. 0	0. 0	0. 3	0. 3	0. 3	46. 5	25. 5	38. 2	46. 8	25. 8	38. 5
India	5. 3	5. 2	22. 7	5. 3	3. 4	13. 7	8. 6	19. 0	13. 0	19. 2	27. 6	49. 4
Indonesia	0. 4	0. 0	(b)	6. 3	27. 7	11. 9	2. 3	6. 2	11. 7	9. 0	33. 9	23. 6
Malaya	(b)	0. 4	11. 5	10. 3	11. 5	22. 9	6. 4	4. 2	7. 8	16. 7	16. 1	42. 2
Pakistan	3. 6	(b)	0. 0	3. 9	5. 2	4. 5	26. 1	31. 7	15. 9	33. 6	36. 9	20. 4
Philippines	0. 0	0. 0	n. a.	0. 0	0. 0	n.a.	0. 0	0. 0	n.a.	0. 0	0. 0	n.a.
Thailand	(b)	0. 0	(b)	0. 1	0. 0	(b)	(b)	0. 0	1. 2	0. 1	0. 0	1. 2
Subtotal	9. 3	20. 8	45. 6	26. 2	58. 6	62. 2	90. 0	104. 1	102. 2	125. 5	183. 5	210. 0
LATIN AMERICA												
Argentina	36. 4	29. 7	16. 5	47. 7	54. 2	18. 6	0. 0	1. 0	0. 8	84. 1	84. 9	35. 9
Brazil	0. 0	0. 7	0. 0	21. 5	41. 3	38. 8	2. 6	4. 6	0. 7	24. 0	46. 6	39. 5
Chile	0. 0	0. 0	0. 0	2. 0	0. 3	(b)	0. 0	(b)	(b)	2. 0	0. 3	(b)
Colombia	0. 0	0. 8	0. 4	0. 0	0. 4	0. 3	0. 0	0. 0	0. 0	0. 0	1. 2	0. 7
Cuba	0. 8	36. 4	14. 2	0. 0	1. 3	3. 1	1. 2	0. 4	(b)	2. 0	38. 1	17. 3
Mexico	(b)	0. 4	0. 0	(b)	(b)	0. 1	(b)	0. 2	2. 0	0. 1	0. 6	2. 1
Peru	0. 0	(b)	0. 0	0. 0	(b)	(b)	(b)	(b)	(b)	(b)	(b)	(b)
Uruguay	0. 0	4. 6	0. 5	3. 8	5. 9	7. 4	(b)	0. 0	[c] 0. 1	23. 7	10. 5	[c] 8. 0
Venezuela	19. 9	0. 0	0. 0	0. 0	0. 0	0. 2	0. 0	0. 0	0. 0	0. 0	0. 0	0. 2
Subtotal	57. 1	72. 6	31. 6	75. 0	103. 4	68. 5	3. 8	6. 2	3. 6	135. 9	182. 2	103. 7
Total	132. 8	181. 4	184. 9	214. 7	334. 5	357. 9	106. 0	135. 8	138. 7	453. 5	651. 7	681. 5

Source: U. S. Department of Commerce.

[a] These data are based on the official trade statistics of the free-world countries involved, that is, the bloc imports indicated are the free-world trading partners' reported exports. Generally, free-world exports are reported on a f. o. b. basis. All values have been rounded to the nearest tenth of a million dollars. A "zero" entry indicates that no figure for trade is known, although some trade may have taken place. Because of rounding, figures do not necessarily add to the totals shown.

[b] Less than $50,000.

[c] Does not include wool known to have been shipped via the Netherlands, amounting to at least $6 million.

n. a.—not available.

TABLE 7. *Sino-Soviet Bloc Exports to Selected Less Developed Countries by Area and Country* [a]

1954–56

(Millions of U.S. dollars)

Area and country	U.S.S.R.			European satellites			Communist China			Total Sino-Soviet bloc		
	1954	1955	1956	1954	1955	1956	1954	1955	1956	1954	1955	1956
EUROPE												
Iceland	8. 1	10. 6	14. 8	4. 6	6. 7	8. 9	(b)	(b)	(b)	12. 7	17. 3	23. 7
Spain	0. 0	0. 0	0. 0	0. 1	0. 0	0. 0	(b)	0. 2	(b)	0. 1	0. 2	(b)
Yugoslavia	1. 1	14. 4	70. 4	2. 9	18. 6	34. 6	0. 0	(b)	3. 5	4. 0	33. 0	108. 5
Subtotal	9. 2	25. 0	85. 2	7. 6	25. 3	43. 5	(b)	0. 2	3. 5	16. 8	50. 5	132. 2
NEAR EAST AND AFRICA												
Egypt	6. 7	6. 6	22. 7	19. 5	28. 2	42. 9	0. 8	0. 9	11. 1	27. 0	35. 7	76. 7
Ghana	(b)	(b)	(b)	2. 9	4. 9	4. 8	(b)	(c)	0. 1	2. 9	4. 9	4. 9
Greece	1. 5	1. 9	4. 8	7. 8	11. 1	16. 6	(b)	0. 1	0. 1	9. 3	13. 1	21. 5
Iran	13. 5	20. 3	17. 5	7. 7	5. 5	9. 0	0. 0	0. 0	0. 0	21. 2	25. 8	26. 5
Iraq	(b)	(c)	(b)	3. 7	5. 1	6. 3	0. 0	0. 1	0. 0	3. 7	5. 2	6. 3
Israel	6. 5	4. 8	0. 4	5. 3	5. 7	3. 3	(b)	(b)	(b)	11. 8	10. 5	3. 7
Jordan	0. 0	(b)	0. 2	1. 9	2. 3	3. 6	(b)	(b)	0. 0	1. 9	2. 3	3. 8
Lebanon	0. 1	0. 8	1. 5	4. 9	5. 2	6. 1	0. 0	0. 2	0. 0	5. 1	6. 2	7. 6
Morocco	0. 3	0. 1	0. 1	2. 6	3. 7	4. 6	11. 1	19. 0	19. 8	14. 0	22. 8	24. 5
Sudan	0. 2	0. 1	0. 4	10. 9	3. 9	6. 7	0. 1	0. 1	0. 3	11. 2	4. 1	7. 4
Syria	0. 1	0. 2	0. 9	4. 4	5. 1	11. 3	0. 2	0. 2	0. 5	4. 8	5. 5	12. 7
Turkey	3. 4	8. 3	5. 2	41. 6	83. 0	54. 2	(b)	0. 0	0. 0	45. 0	91. 3	59. 4
Subtotal	32. 3	43. 1	53. 7	113. 2	163. 7	169. 4	12. 2	20. 6	31. 9	157. 7	227. 4	255. 0
SOUTH AND SOUTHEAST ASIA												
Burma	0. 1	0. 1	3. 1	2. 3	1. 6	12. 2	0. 5	2. 3	22. 2	3. 0	4. 0	37. 5
Ceylon	0. 4	0. 1	0. 2	0. 6	1. 5	1. 4	32. 0	16. 8	28. 1	33. 1	18. 4	29. 7
India	2. 4	6. 0	31. 3	4. 0	9. 1	20. 9	4. 8	8. 0	20. 1	11. 2	23. 2	72. 3
Indochina	(b)	(d)	(d)	0. 4	(d)	(d)	8. 9	(d)	(d)	9. 3	(d)	(d)
Indonesia	0. 6	0. 2	0. 3	11. 2	30. 2	14. 2	3. 5	9. 9	30. 2	15. 3	40. 3	44. 7
Malaya	(b)	(b)	0. 1	4. 3	4. 1	5. 2	28. 5	37. 8	43. 1	32. 7	41. 9	48. 3
Pakistan	0. 2	0. 1	0. 3	2. 6	3. 0	1. 0	3. 7	0. 4	[e] 7. 4	6. 5	3. 4	[e] 8. 7
Philippines	0. 0	0. 0	0. 0	0. 2	(b)	(b)	0. 9	0. 4	(b)	1. 1	0. 4	(c)
Thailand	0. 2	0. 1	(b)	1. 6	0. 9	2. 0	2. 9	0. 0	(b)	4. 6	1. 0	2. 0
Viet-Nam	(f)	0. 0	0. 1	(f)	0. 0	0. 0	(f)	9. 1	4. 1	(f)	9. 1	4. 2
Subtotal	3. 9	6. 6	35. 4	27. 2	50. 4	56. 9	85. 7	84. 7	155. 2	116. 8	141. 7	247. 4

TABLE 7. *Sino-Soviet Bloc Exports to Selected Less Developed Countries by Area and Country* [a]—Continued

1954–56

(Millions of U.S. dollars)

Area and country	U.S.S.R.			European satellites			Communist China			Total Sino-Soviet bloc		
	1954	1955	1956	1954	1955	1956	1954	1955	1956	1954	1955	1956
LATIN AMERICA												
Argentina	36. 7	32. 2	26. 7	40. 0	71. 4	28. 5	(b)	0. 0	0. 0	76. 7	103. 6	55. 2
Brazil	0. 0	0. 0	0. 0	18. 8	38. 1	46. 1	0. 0	0. 0	0. 0	18. 8	38. 1	46. 1
Chile	0. 0	0. 0	(b)	0. 1	1. 2	2. 3	0. 0	1. 3	0. 8	0. 1	2. 5	3. 1
Colombia	(b)	0. 0	0. 0	1. 4	1. 2	1. 2	(c)	(b)	0. 0	1. 4	1. 2	1. 2
Cuba	0. 0	0. 0	0. 0	0. 8	1. 3	2. 6	0. 0	0. 0	(b)	0. 8	1. 3	2. 6
Mexico	(b)	(b)	0. 1	1. 0	1. 0	2. 0	0. 4	0. 3	0. 6	1. 4	1. 3	2. 7
Peru	0. 0	(b)	0. 0	(b)	0. 1	0. 6	0. 1	0. 1	(b)	0. 1	0. 2	0. 6
Uruguay	(b)	0. 1	3. 2	2. 5	2. 4	7. 4	0. 0	(b)	(b)	2. 5	2. 5	10. 6
Venezuela	0. 1	(b)	0. 1	1. 6	1. 9	2. 5	0. 1	0. 1	0. 1	1. 8	2. 0	2. 7
Subtotal	36. 8	32. 3	30. 1	66. 2	118. 6	93. 1	0. 6	1. 8	1. 5	103. 6	152. 7	124. 8
Total	82. 2	107. 0	204. 4	214. 2	358. 0	364. 9	98. 5	107. 3	192. 1	394. 9	572. 3	759. 4

Source: U. S. Department of Commerce.

[a] These data are based on the official trade statistics of the free-world countries involved, that is, the bloc exports indicated are the free-world trading partners' reported imports. Generally, free-world imports are reported on a c. i. f. basis. All values have been rounded to the nearest tenth of a million dollars. A "zero" entry indicates that no figure for trade is known, although some trade may have taken place. Because of rounding, figures do not necessarily add to the totals shown.

[b] Less than $50,000.

[c] Less than $100,000.

[d] Beginning in 1955, trade statistics for Indochina are reported separately by the three independent countries of the area.

[e] This figure includes $6.9 million of imports from Communist China on government account, not reported in the statistics.

[f] Reported under Indochina for 1954.

TABLE 8. *Exports of Selected Less Developed Countries to the Sino-Soviet Bloc as Percent of the Countries' Total Exports*

Country	1956	1955	1954	1953	1947
Iceland	30. 0	27. 8	24. 9	19. 8	5. 8
Yugoslavia	24. 2	13. 8	2. 6	--------	52. 8
Egypt	34. 4	26. 7	14. 2	12. 2	6. 2
Ghana	2. 4	4. 2	6. 3	4. 0	2. 0
Greece	10. 4	4. 6	7. 1	6. 3	5. 8
Iran	16. 7	9. 5	18. 2	12. 5	5. 0
Israel	4. 6	3. 9	5. 2	3. 4	1. 8
Jordan	5. 9	7. 3	negligible	--------	----------
Lebanon	6. 0	6. 2	2. 3	2. 0	----------
Sudan	3. 2	2. 9	0. 8	0. 1	0. 4
Syria	7. 8	1. 2	0. 5	--------	----------
Turkey	19. 6	21. 9	16. 5	7. 4	7. 2

TABLE 8. *Exports of Selected Less Developed Countries to the Sino-Soviet Bloc as Percent of the Countries' Total Exports*—Continued

Country	1956	1955	1954	1953	1947
Burma	14.3	19.0	negligible	1.3	7.3
Ceylon	10.6	6.3	12.3	15.6	negligible
India	4.0	2.2	1.6	1.3	4.6
Indonesia	2.7	3.6	1.2	0.5	1.0
Malaya	3.1	1.2	1.6	1.6	3.4
Pakistan	6.0	8.1	9.4	4.5	----------
Argentina	4.4	8.9	8.8	2.1	1.4
Brazil	2.7	3.3	1.5	0.7	4.3
Cuba	2.4	6.4	0.4	0.1	0.1
Uruguay	3.8	5.7	9.5	0.4	5.5

Source: U.S. Department of Commerce.

TABLE 9. *Imports of Selected Less Developed Countries From the Sino-Soviet Bloc as Percent of the Countries' Total Imports*

Country	1956	1955	1954	1953	1947
Iceland	26.3	22.2	18.3	8.6	6.9
Yugoslavia	23.0	7.5	1.2	--------	56.3
Egypt	14.4	6.8	5.9	7.7	4.0
Ghana	2.0	2.1	1.5	1.1	2.7
Greece	4.6	3.5	2.8	1.3	3.5
Iran	9.7	9.4	9.5	9.7	13.0
Iraq	2.0	1.9	1.8	3.1	1.8
Jordan	5.3	3.0	3.4	2.2	1.5
Lebanon	3.7	2.6	2.3	1.9	--------
Morocco	5.5	4.9	2.9	--------	--------
Sudan	5.7	3.0	8.0	2.4	0.9
Syria	3.9	2.8	2.5	3.3	--------
Turkey	14.6	18.4	9.4	5.5	6.4
Burma	18.9	2.3	1.5	1.3	--------
Ceylon	8.7	6.0	11.3	13.5	0.5
India	4.3	1.7	0.9	0.7	1.2
Indonesia	5.2	6.7	2.4	0.9	4.8
Malaya	3.6	3.4	3.2	3.8	9.3
Pakistan	3.1	1.2	2.0	1.2	--------
Viet-Nam	2.0	3.5	--------	--------	--------
Argentina	5.3	9.5	7.1	1.8	1.2
Brazil	3.7	2.9	1.1	0.8	0.6
Uruguay	5.2	1.1	0.9	0.4	0.7

Source: U.S. Department of Commerce.

The trade of the European satellites, in contrast to that of the Soviets, is characterized by the export of more machinery and equipment and other highly elaborated goods in exchange for raw materials and agricultural products. On the other hand, nearly 60 percent of Communist China's exports to the underdeveloped countries consisted of raw materials and food products, while these same classes of goods accounted for 80 percent of its imports from these areas. This trade pattern has remained approximately unchanged since 1953, although it is noteworthy that exports of manufactured goods rose from about $11 million to nearly $55 million. These manufactured goods consisted, in increasing amounts, of cotton textiles and other light industry products, cement, chemicals, and steel products. These changes indicate that the industrialization program being pushed in Communist China has had some impact on the trade with Asia.

Trade Agreements. The bloc trade offensive has been spearheaded by a campaign to expand its network of trade agreements with the less developed countries. These agreements establish the official framework and conditions for the conduct of trade. They usually express the willingness of both parties to engage in trade, establish the types of commodities to be exchanged, sometimes set target quotas for these items, and arrange for the means of payment—frequently through clearing accounts. Individual transactions within this framework are worked out by negotiation.

The bloc's bilateral trade and payments agreements with free-world less developed countries totaled 147 at the end of 1957 as compared with 49 at the end of 1953 (see Table 10, p. 40). Czechoslovakia led the list of bloc countries with 26 agreements signed; the U.S.S.R. has 20 agreements. On the side of the less developed countries, India had the most agreements with bloc countries (see Table 11, p. 41).

In its trade with the less developed countries, the Soviet Union generally seeks through trade agreements to maintain a bilateral balance. This is accomplished either by advance agreement as to the value of goods to be mutually delivered (e. g., with Afghanistan and Iran), or by agreement that the U.S.S.R. will use the proceeds of its exports for purchases in the importing country (e. g., with India). The U.S.S.R. also uses bilateral clearing accounts for this purpose (e. g., with Egypt, Syria, and Lebanon).

In 1956 about 99 percent of all Soviet exports to the less developed countries and about 80 percent of its imports from those countries was carried on with countries with which the Soviet Union had trade or payments agreements, or both. The balance on the import side consisted mainly of purchases of sugar in Cuba, rubber in Malaya, and cocoa in Ghana. With regard to the European satellites about 91 percent of their imports from and 85 percent of their exports to less developed countries involved countries with which they maintained trade or payments agreements, or both. The corresponding figures for Communist China were 76 percent of imports and 61 percent of exports.

It is difficult to make an overall judgment on performance under bloc trade agreements. About half of the agreements with the less developed countries do not provide for specific targets for volume, and in any event, sales contracts may be concluded outside the scope of the agreements. However, in most of the cases where trade targets have been stated, actual levels of trade have fallen short of the specified amounts. Nevertheless, the agreements are important as an indication of intentions and have generally been followed up by significant increases in trade. They have also had considerable propaganda value, particularly at the time of their first announcement.

TABLE 10.—*Trade and Payments Agreements in Force Between the Sino-Soviet Bloc and the Less Developed Countries, December 31, 1953–December 31, 1957* [a]

Area and country	Estimated number as of December 31, 1957		Estimated number as of December 31, 1956	Estimated number as of December 31, 1955	Estimated number as of December 31, 1954	Estimated number as of December 31, 1953
	Number	Increase over 1953				
SOUTH ASIA						
Afghanistan	4	3	3	2	2	1
Ceylon	6	5	6	3	1	1
India	10	6	9	8	8	4
Pakistan	4	4	4	0	0	0
Subtotal	24	18	22	13	11	6
SOUTHEAST ASIA						
Burma	7	7	8	6	1	0
Cambodia	4	4	2	0	0	0
Indonesia	9	6	6	6	6	3
Subtotal	20	17	16	12	7	3
NEAR EAST AND AFRICA						
Egypt	[b] 9	3	8	8	7	6
Ethiopia	1	1	1	0	0	0
Greece	7	2	7	7	7	5
Iran	4	0	4	4	4	4
Israel	5	3	5	5	5	2
Lebanon	8	7	8	4	3	1
Morocco	[c] 5	5	0	0	0	0
Sudan	4	4	4	4	0	0
Syria	9	8	8	4	1	1
Tunisia	3	3	0	0	0	0
Turkey	7	3	7	7	6	4
Yemen	5	5	3	0	0	0
Subtotal	67	44	55	43	33	23
LATIN AMERICA						
Argentina	5	0	5	6	6	5
Brazil	3	1	3	3	3	2
Colombia	2	2	1	1	0	0
Mexico	1	0	1	1	1	1
Paraguay	3	1	3	3	2	2
Uruguay	6	3	6	5	5	3
Subtotal	20	7	19	19	17	13
EUROPE						
Iceland	6	2	6	6	6	4
Spain	1	1	0	0	0	0
Yugoslavia	9	9	9	8	1	0
Subtotal	16	12	15	14	7	4
Grand total	147	98	127	101	75	49

[a] Insofar as possible this table attempts to show agreements known to be in effect on December 31 of each year. Due to incomplete data, however, the list also includes agreements which are assumed to have been tacitly renewed as well as newly signed agreements of uncertain date of entry into force.

[b] The Egyptian-North Viet-Nam agreement is not included since it enters into force on January 1, 1958.

[c] The Moroccan-Polish agreement is not included since it enters into force on January 1, 1958.

Table 11. *Trade and/or Payments Agreements Between the Sino-Soviet Bloc and the Less Developed Countries as of December 31, 1957*

Area and country	Alba-nia	Bul-garia	Czech-oslo-vakia	East Ger-many	Hun-gary	Pol-and	Ruma-nia	U.S.S.R.	China	North Korea	North Viet-Nam	Total
Europe												
Iceland			TP	TP	TP	TP	TP	TP				6
Spain						TP						1
Yugoslavia	TP	TP	TP	TP	TP	TP	TP	TP	TP			9
Near East and Africa												
Egypt		TP	TP	TP	TP	TP	TP	TP	TP	TP		9
Ethiopia			TP									1
Greece		TP	TP	TP	TP	TP	TP	TP				7
Iran			TP		TP	TP		TP				4
Israel		TP			TP	TP	TP	P				5
Lebanon		T	TP	TP	T	TP	TP	TP	T			8
Morocco		T	T		T			T	T			5
Sudan			P	P	P	P						4
Syria	TP	T	T	TP	T	TP	TP	TP	TP			9
Tunisia		TP	TP					TP				3
Turkey		TP	TP	TP	TP	TP	TP	TP				7
Yemen			T	TP		T	T	T				5
South and Southeast Asia												
Afghanistan			TP			TP		TP	TP			4
Burma		T	TP	TP	TP		T	TP		T		7
Cambodia			TP			TP		TP	TP			4
Ceylon		TP	TP		TP	TP	TP		TP			6
India		T	T	T	T	T	T	T	T	T	T	10
Indonesia			T	T	T	T	T	T	TP	T	T	9
Pakistan			T		T	T		T				4
Latin America												
Argentina			TP		TP	TP	TP	TP				5
Brazil			TP		TP	TP						3
Colombia			TP	TP								2
Mexico			TP									1
Paraguay			P		P	P						3
Uruguay		P	P	P	P	P		P				6
Total	2	13	26	14	20	22	14	20	10	4	2	147

TP—Trade and Payments Agreement.
T—Trade Agreement only. All payments are made on a cash basis and no clearing account is maintained.
P—Payments Agreement only. In some cases there are, nevertheless, commodities and quotas.

Other Trade Promotion. Another important form of bloc trade promotion is participation in trade fairs. It has been estimated that in 1955 the bloc spent about $9 million for this purpose in the less developed countries, nearly

$3 million in India alone. Czechoslovakia was the largest single exhibitor, with the U.S.S.R. next in importance. The U.S.S.R. has also staged a number of large-scale exhibitions, including those at Djakarta in 1954; Kabul, Izmir, Damascus, and Djakarta in 1956; and Cairo in 1957.

As part of the offensive, Soviet and other bloc countries have also become increasingly active in exchanging commercial, agricultural, and industrial delegations with less developed countries of the free world.

Assistance Agreements as a Factor in Future Trade. As previously indicated, the provisions of bloc assistance agreements constitute a strong continuing link between the bloc creditor and the recipient country. Over the next few years deliveries of equipment and supplies for bloc projects will raise trade considerably. Thereafter, to the extent that commodities are accepted by the bloc countries in repayment for credits, the bloc will become an increasingly important outlet for the major export products of the countries which have accepted its assistance. This relationship will extend for many years, particularly in the cases involving Soviet credits. Unless there are substantial increases in the production of major export commodities, the commitment of exports to the bloc will, of course, tend to reduce correspondingly the ability of the underdeveloped countries to purchase goods from the traditional free-world suppliers. Moreover, where heavy commitments to the bloc are involved, repayments may jeopardize existing trade channels and outlets in the free world, thus progressively increasing the debtor countries' dependence on the bloc and strengthening the Soviet's hand in dealing with them.

Character of Bloc Trade. The recurrent problem of many less developed countries in disposing of their principal export commodities in their traditional markets at prices they consider satisfactory has given the bloc opportunities to exploit trade relations as a tool of diplomacy. It has taken advantage of Burma's temporary rice surplus, Egypt's cotton disposal problem, and Iceland's difficulty in marketing its fish to increase its economic relations with these countries, and has recently tried to arrange a tie-in barter and aid deal for Sudan's cotton. Resentment of restrictive features of Western commercial policies is exploited by Soviet propaganda, which also plays upon the widespread feeling that the Western developed countries can somehow manipulate the terms of trade to the disadvantage of exporters of primary products. The bloc, with its Socialist economies, is pictured, by contrast, as willing and able to pay what it calls "just" prices and, despite its past record, to provide stable markets.

While bloc offers are tempting to countries faced with temporary marketing difficulties for their basic export products, and while the bloc has stepped in on several occasions to make significant bilateral deals, this type of trade with the bloc presents certain drawbacks, many of which may only become apparent to the country at some later time. Under this type of barter, the less developed country loses the valuable independence of choice of imports of goods and services necessary to economic development, which only trade with free-market countries affords. Furthermore, the expected improvement in the terms of trade may be illusory. In some cases prices for bloc goods have been higher than for those of traditional suppliers. For example, in Burma, a top level official publicly stated that the barter deal with the U.S.S.R. ultimately resulted in a 10 to 30 percent price disadvantage to his country. When the price of rice rose on the free market, Burma sought and finally obtained relief from the U.S.S.R. on its commitments and Burmese-Soviet trade fell off in 1956 and 1957. Uruguay accepted Polish coal at a considerably higher price than the world market in order to use its clearing balance with that country.

The U.S.S.R's willingness to provide types of goods in short supply internally has been confined mainly to cases in which political considerations were paramount. Thus, some of the less developed countries have found themselves with substantial export balances with the U.S.S.R. because the Soviets are unwilling or unable to provide the types of import goods which these countries wish to purchase. For example, Argentina and Burma both found themselves with substantial bloc trade credits which they could not use for the types and quantities of goods which they required. Moreover, while traditional Western suppliers have facilities for providing expeditiously the servicing and spare parts which are essential for most lines of machinery and equipment, there have been complaints against the U.S.S.R. in this regard.

Politically inspired bloc purchases at prices higher than those prevailing on the world market—and given the nature of the state trading system the bloc can offer such prices relatively easily—result in the diversion of trade and over time lead to the gradual drying up of traditional market outlets and export trade channels. This has already occurred to some extent in the case of Egyptian cotton. Moreover, while the bloc could absorb considerable quantities of imported food and raw materials if it wished to do so, large-scale purchases frequently present the bloc with at least short run problems of processing capacity, storage or utilization, not to mention the problem of balancing foreign exchange revenues and outlays. Such difficulties may explain why the bloc has offered for resale at discount prices in free-world markets commodities purchased from some of the less developed countries, for example, Egyptian cotton and Burmese rice.

There are still other drawbacks for countries using the bloc as a source of supply. These stem from the nature of Soviet-type planning systems, which are plagued by rigidities and inefficiencies, often acute in the trade field. The famous example of Soviet cement shipments to Burma, unloaded in Rangoon just before the monsoon season despite Burmese protestations, had its counterpart in Egypt, where a large cement order was not delivered until after the need for it had passed. Crude oil shipments to Egypt had a high sulphur content and damaged refinery facilities. Wheat shipments to Egypt were late in delivery and of lower quality than specified. East German cars and Soviet trucks had to be shipped back from Syria due to poor quality; complaints about Czechoslovak and Soviet automotive equipment were registered in Argentina, Greece, Afghanistan, and Indonesia. Complaints against bloc steel products were made in Egypt and Uruguay. Even bloc spokesmen have alluded, with typical double-talk, to Soviet failures of this kind. Thus, Khrushchev in his Kiev speech of December 24, 1956, stated that "constant control must also be exerted to insure that our industry fulfills on time and properly all orders placed by foreign countries."

Part Two

The Bloc Economic Offensive in Individual Countries

V. THE NEAR EAST

Egypt

Since mid-1955, Egypt has been a major target of the Sino-Soviet bloc economic offensive. However, there was already a historical basis of economic relations between the Soviet-bloc countries and Egypt, as evidenced by the fact that in 1938 approximately 10 percent of Egypt's total trade was with countries now comprising the Sino-Soviet bloc. As early as 1949 Egypt had bilateral trade agreements with several countries in the Soviet orbit, and in 1953 the U.S.S.R. signed its first payments agreement with Egypt. Through barter agreements signed in 1951 and 1953, bloc countries undertook to ship wheat to Egypt in exchange for cotton. The Soviet bloc significantly strengthened its economic ties with Egypt in 1954, during which year the U.S.S.R. and Rumania capitalized upon Egypt's price dispute with Western petroleum suppliers by signing the first of the barter agreements involving an exchange of petroleum products for cotton.

The Soviet-bloc economic offensive took more definite shape in 1955, as a consequence of Egypt's difficulty in marketing its cotton in the West and as an outgrowth of Egypt's desire for arms. The Egyptian economy depends heavily upon exports of cotton as its source of foreign exchange, and the poor marketing prospects in 1955 threatened to precipitate a serious deficit in Egypt's current international transactions. Soviet-bloc countries seized upon this situation as a means of strengthening their position in Egypt by offering to purchase much larger quantities of cotton. The desire for arms on the part of Egypt brought the Soviet-bloc offensive clearly into the open and led to the conclusion of the large Soviet-Egyptian arms deal of September 1955. The consummation of this agreement was facilitated by the fact that the U.S.S.R. agreed to accept cotton in repayment of the credit for arms.

Whereas Egypt's need to market its cotton plus its desire for arms helped to produce a climate generally favorable to the Sino-Soviet economic offensive, political motivations growing out of President Gamel Abdel Nasser's "positive neutralism" also constituted a contributory factor. In its international economic relations Egypt presumably sought to reduce its dependence upon the West by expanding its dealings with the bloc. The anti-Western feeling generated by the creation of Israel tended to strengthen this desire.

Although not initially a determining factor, Egypt's urgent need for economic development has also encouraged bloc economic overtures. Egypt has a population of more than 23 million persons who are primarily dependent upon the productivity of roughly 6 million acres of land. The only way it can hope even to maintain the presently low level of income (approximately $110 per capita annually) is to expand agricultural acreage wherever feasible and to promote a greater degree of industrialization. The pursuance of such objectives depends not only upon a favorable export market for cotton, but also upon a sizable inflow of long-term capital. As early as 1955 the Soviet bloc endeavored to capitalize on this situation by offering economic assistance to Egypt in general terms. However, none of these earlier offers resulted in serious negotiations until late in 1957. The U.S.S.R. credit offer of about $175 million for industrial development, accepted in principle in November 1957, resulted in the aid agreement of January 1958.

Credits and Grants. Aside from a gift of approximately $2.8 million by the Soviet Red Cross in November 1956, the Soviet bloc has made no significant grants to Egypt. The reported grant of 20 million Swiss francs ($4 million) by Communist China in early 1956 may have been related to settlement of Peiping's large clearing-account deficit with Egypt.

Until recently Soviet-bloc offers to help Egyptian economic development resulted only in contracts for a few specific projects, most of which probably did not involve any bloc credits. So far as is known, only the Czechoslovak offer of late 1955 to construct a ceramics factory in Egypt at a cost of roughly $1 million has involved any bloc credit. Other reported contracts, including a cement plant (Czechoslovakia), a nuclear physics laboratory (U.S.S.R.), and various bridges (Hungary and Czechoslovakia) and power stations (East Germany and Hungary), are presumably commercial agreements involving little if any Soviet-bloc credit.

Even prior to the recent economic development credit agreements with the U.S.S.R. and Czechoslovakia a number of grandiose offers had been reported. During 1954 Egyptian sources reported that the Soviet Union had offered to assist Egypt in the construction of the High Aswan Dam. These offers were allegedly repeated in 1955, and in June 1956 the U.S.S.R. again was reported to have offered to lend Egypt $1.2 billion for the construction of the High Aswan Dam as well as for other projects. It is by no means clear, however, whether or not these reported overtures constituted firm offers on the part of the U.S.S.R. On July 21, 1956, the Soviet Foreign Minister, Dmitri T. Shepilov, was quoted as stating that the U.S.S.R. was not considering aid to Egypt for construction of the dam.

Following the withdrawal of the Western offer to assist in the building of the High Aswan Dam in 1956, the U.S.S.R. seemingly retreated from these earlier alleged offers and suggested that it might help Egypt with less spectacular projects. In line with this position the Soviet Ambassador to Egypt in early 1957 tentatively offered to assist Egypt in the realization of the newly announced industrialization program. On November 19 Soviet Premier Nikolai Bulganin announced that in response to a request by President Nasser the U.S.S.R. had agreed to help Egypt develop its economy. Specifically, the U.S.S.R. reportedly offered to lend up to 700 million rubles (approximately $175 million) for use in implementing Egypt's industrialization program. Shortly thereafter Czechoslovakia allegedly agreed to extend to Egypt a loan of $56 million for economic development. In January 1958 Egyptian Minister of Economy Sidqi headed a delegation to Moscow to work out details relating to the Soviet offer. On January 29, 1958, agreement was reportedly reached, whereby the U.S.S.R.

was to provide Egypt with technical assistance, equipment, and machinery up to a cost of $178 million. The types of projects contemplated include iron smelters, steel fabricating plants, shipyards, textile mills, and other enterprises. Some of the equipment for these projects is to be furnished by the European satellites. Repayment of the Soviet credit will reportedly take place over a 12-year period at 2.5 percent interest. The recent Soviet and Czechoslovak credits, if fully utilized, will provide about half of the estimated foreign exchange cost pertaining to Egypt's $700 million industrialization program. The effect of the recent political union between Egypt and Syria on this agreement is not yet clear, although press reports have quoted Egyptian officials as stating that the Soviet loans to Syria and Egypt would now be considered as one.

Since few projects undertaken by Soviet-bloc countries in Egypt are under way, reaction to performance has been limited. No significant criticism of Czechoslovak, Soviet, or Polish firms on the part of the Egyptian Government has been noted. On the other hand Egypt is clearly disappointed with Hungarian performance on contracts to supply bridges and a thermoelectric power plant.

Up to the present time the sale of arms on credit has probably been the most important aspect of the Soviet economic offensive in Egypt. The first report of the Soviet arms transactions with Egypt came in September 1955. The basic agreement was probably reached during the visit of Shepilov to Egypt in the summer of 1955. Arms continued to be shipped during 1956, presumably under a supplemental agreement. Following the cessation of Suez hostilities in late 1956 the U.S.S.R. resumed its deliveries of arms to Egypt. There is no precise

Egyptian crowd inspects a Soviet bomber supplied by the U.S.S.R. to the United Arab Republic.

information available concerning the cost of these arms, but reports indicate that the amount of Egyptian indebtedness was at least $250 million, and possibly considerably more. However, there are indications that the U.S.S.R. may have considerably reduced this indebtedness. The agreement permitted Egypt to pay for these arms over a period of at least 5 years in either cotton or foreign exchange. The purchase of these arms has doubtless obligated a significant percentage of Egypt's cotton over the next few years.

Virtually every kind of conventional military equipment for land, sea, and air forces has been shipped to Egypt under the arms agreements. Much of this materiel was lost during the period of the 1956 hostilities, but subsequent deliveries probably more than offset this loss.

Technical Assistance. In pursuing its economic offensive in Egypt the Soviet bloc has laid considerable stress upon technical assistance and training. Although Egypt has a larger supply of technical experts, especially agricultural technicians, than most countries of the Middle East, there are serious deficiencies in some fields, particularly heavy industry. Soviet-bloc offers of economic assistance have usually included proposals to supply industrial and mining experts, and the U.S.S.R. has shown a continuing interest in assisting Egypt in petroleum exploration.

Egypt has not accepted any of the general offers of technical assistance, and there are indications that the Egyptian Government will endeavor to limit the number of Soviet technicians entering the country under the recent economic aid agreement with the U.S.S.R. Most of the technicians who have come to Egypt in the past 2 years have been primarily concerned with the implementation of various construction contracts held by bloc firms. It is estimated that during the last 6 months of 1957 more than 360 Soviet-bloc nonmilitary technicians were in Egypt for 1 month or more. Of this total almost two-thirds came from the U.S.S.R., Czechoslovakia, and East Germany. Their purpose in coming to Egypt was to assist in the construction of an atomic research laboratory, a power plant, bridges, oil storage tanks, and various other projects. The Egyptian Government has indicated some reluctance to increase the number of Soviet-bloc technicians, particularly in connection with the implementation of the recent credits.

Some Egyptians have gone to bloc countries for technical training. Bloc countries have readily offered to provide such training; and the U.S.S.R., Czechoslovakia, East Germany, and Poland extend scholarships to Egyptian nationals. In addition to such trainees Egyptian delegations have visited Soviet-bloc countries to observe industrial installations and agricultural operations.

Since the conclusion of the Soviet arms agreement with Egypt in September 1955, a substantial number of Soviet-bloc military technicians have been assigned to the country. During the last 6 months of 1957 it is believed that more than 450 Soviet-bloc military specialists went to Egypt for the purpose of training military personnel and of supervising the construction of military installations. More than 100 such technical experts have reportedly been assigned to the Egyptian Air Force as instructors. Egypt has also sent its military personnel to bloc countries for training, and during calendar year 1957 these trainees numbered as many as 500, a large percentage of whom were receiving flight training.

Trade. In recent years cotton has accounted for from 70 to 80 percent of Egypt's total exports. Until about 2 years ago Western Europe and India were by far the most important buyers of Egyptian cotton, and the former region also supplied the bulk of Egypt's import requirements. Countries now comprising the Sino-Soviet bloc accounted for less than 15 percent of Egypt's total trade until 1955.

The Western demand for Egyptian cotton has generally tended to weaken in the post-World War II period, but moderate increases in purchases by other countries, including the Soviet bloc, helped to offset the Western decline. In 1955, however, the drop in exports to the West threatened to intensify seriously Egypt's chronic trade deficit. To exploit this situation the Sino-Soviet bloc began to increase substantially its imports of Egyptian cotton.

Egypt's exports to the Sino-Soviet bloc in recent years, as compared with its total exports, are illustrated in the following table (in millions of Egyptian pounds):

Year	*Sino-Soviet bloc*	*World*	*Percentage to bloc*
1938	2. 8	29. 3	10
1950	16. 4	173. 0	9
1952	25. 4	142. 9	18
1954	19. 6	136. 7	14
1955	36. 9	137. 0	27
1956	48. 5	140. 9	34
1957 (11 months)	66. 5	145. 9	46

During 1955 India and France continued to be the two leading buyers of Egyptian cotton, but their position was threatened by Czechoslovakia, Communist China, and the U.S.S.R. Payment for arms may have partly accounted for this substantial rise in exports to the bloc during 1955, but these exports had already reached sizable proportions before the arms agreement was signed. The two trade agreements signed with Communist China in August 1955 definitely accounted for the large-scale increase in exports to the country. In 1956 Soviet-bloc countries continued their large purchases of Egyptian cotton, whereas Egypt's exports to the West dropped sharply after the nationalization of the Suez Canal in July 1956.

During 1956 Czechoslovakia became Egypt's most important export market. The aftermath of the Suez crisis seriously curtailed Egypt's trade with Western Europe during much of 1957, and normal trade relations with France and the United Kingdom had not yet been resumed in early 1958. Meanwhile, the Sino-Soviet bloc countries continued to increase their imports of Egyptian goods, and accounted for nearly 50 percent of Egypt's total exports in 1957; the U.S.S.R. was by far Egypt's most important market.

Egypt's imports from the Sino-Soviet bloc have lagged considerably behind exports. During 1955, for example, Egypt continued to buy most of its needs in the free world, despite its drop in exports to that area. Consequently, in its trade relations with the bloc Egypt has regularly enjoyed a sizable trade surplus. After July 1956 imports from the bloc tended to increase largely because Egypt lacked the foreign exchange resources with which to maintain its normal flow of goods from Western countries. Egypt's imports from the Sino-Soviet bloc in recent years are shown in the table below (in millions of Egyptian pounds):

Year	Sino-Soviet bloc	World	Percentage from bloc
1938	3. 6	36. 9	10
1950	11. 3	213. 3	5
1952	22. 0	225. 8	10
1954	9. 4	160. 3	6
1955	12. 5	182. 9	7
1956	26. 7	186. 0	14
1957 (11 months)	42. 6	162. 5	26

Egypt's imports from the Sino-Soviet bloc are rather diversified, but petroleum products, wheat, timber and wood, fertilizers, and iron and steel products are especially important. Egypt's large-scale imports of petroleum products from the bloc began in 1954, when a barter agreement was signed with Rumania and the U.S.S.R. Prior to 1956 the U.S.S.R had sometimes shipped wheat to Egypt to offset deficiencies in local output.

The Soviet-bloc countries have used various trade promotion tactics in their relations with Egypt. Most impressive of these from the Egyptian viewpoint have been their willingness to purchase surplus Egyptian cotton at premium prices, their readiness to barter arms for cotton, and their ability to supply Egypt with essential requirements during the period of the Suez crisis. These tactics undoubtedly promoted Egyptian receptivity to closer trade ties with the Soviet bloc.

Other less spectacular tactics have also been employed by the Communist countries in their economic offensive in Egypt. During the past 3 years many Soviet-bloc trade delegations visited Egypt. In 1956 Nikolai Melnokov, chief of Technoexport, the U.S.S.R. foreign trade corporation, visited Egypt during his tour of Middle East countries. Later in the same year Heinrich Rau, the Minister of Foreign Trade for East Germany, headed a delegation that spent several days in Egypt. In the summer of 1955 Dmitri Shepilov, then President of the Foreign Affairs Committee of the Supreme Soviet, visited Egypt to discuss arms shipments and trade between Egypt and the U.S.S.R. In addition to these transient missions several Soviet-bloc countries have negotiated with Egypt to permit the establishment of permanent trade offices. The U.S.S.R., East Germany, and Communist China have established such offices in Cairo.

The bloc has also endeavored to promote its trade relations with Egypt by staging trade fairs and exhibits. As early as 1954 East Germany had an industrial exhibit in Egypt. In April 1956 Communist China staged a trade fair in Egypt, at which it featured textiles, machinery, and various consumer goods. Early in 1957 the U.S.S.R. held a large-scale industrial exhibition in Cairo, where it displayed both capital and consumer goods. Late in 1957 East Germany staged another trade fair in Egypt. Reaction to this fair indicated that it may not have been up to the level of earlier ones. Soviet-bloc states participated in the Egyptian fair of late 1957, and Egyptian delegations have attended trade and industrial fairs held in some Soviet-bloc countries. Aside from these trade fairs and exhibits, Communist countries have endeavored to promote trade relations with Egypt by resorting to mass communication, primarily the press and the radio.

Egypt's trade agreements with Soviet-bloc countries are not uniform as to form and substance. In general, they are bilateral, although Egypt, Rumania, and the U.S.S.R. have a trilateral agreement relating to the shipment of petroleum products to Egypt. The agreements fall into two general categories, trade agreements and payments agreements. In most instances Egypt has signed both types of agreements with the Communist states.

Egypt presently has bilateral trade and/or payments agreements with the U.S.S.R., all European satellites, Communist China, and North Korea. Basic agreements with some of these countries were signed as early as 1949, but the majority have been signed since the beginning of 1955, and they were clearly related to Egypt's desire to expand its markets for cotton. Performance under these agreements varies from country to country, but during the past year trade with some of the more important Communist states has been well above prescribed quotas. However, the bloc's exports to Egypt have not kept pace with its imports, resulting in an Egyptian export surplus with the bloc.

In general, Egypt seems to have been reasonably satisfied with its trade relations with the Soviet-bloc countries. The bloc obtained goodwill by stepping up purchases of cotton in 1955 and in keeping Egypt supplied with wheat and petroleum during the period of the Suez crisis. On the other hand, some dissatisfaction has been noted, which could in the longer run have some bearing on Egypt's trade relations with the bloc. There have been some complaints that bloc deliveries have been slow and that the quality of some goods tends to be inferior. It was felt in some quarters that not all of the wheat imported from the U.S.S.R. came up to specifications, and Egyptians have complained that the high sulfur content in the Soviet crude oil damages Egyptian refinery equipment. There is also apparently some feeling that the Soviet bloc's sporadic buying of Egyptian cotton at premium prices in 1957 discouraged other buyers from entering the market. Persisting reports that Egyptian cotton is being reexported by the bloc to Western Europe has also aroused some concern in official circles. Soviet-bloc countries were unable to provide badly needed pharmaceuticals which were in short supply after the Suez crisis.

Sudan

Although the Sino-Soviet bloc had been making attempts to expand economic relations with the Sudan for several years, it was not until the Sudan got into cotton marketing difficulties in mid-1957 that the bloc was able to make overtures which were intended to have great appeal for the Sudanese. Sudan's vulnerability to these overtures stems from the Sudan's overwhelming dependence on one cash crop, long-staple cotton. Raw cotton comprises about 70 percent of the Sudan's exports and is the chief source of foreign exchange.

Until 1957 the Sudan had never experienced more than normal difficulties in marketing its crop. At the beginning of 1957, prospects for a favorable season were good—a bumper crop had been harvested and prices were relatively high. However, the government's marketing board apparently misjudged the world cotton situation and set its prices at unrealistically high levels, with the result that export sales dropped off drastically. The U.S.S.R. was quick to recognize that this situation provided an opportunity for penetrating the Sudanese economy. In August 1957 it made a token purchase of 9,000 bales of Sudanese cotton, which it followed up by an offer to take large quantities of surplus cotton to be paid for by large-scale economic assistance. The Soviet offer included construction of industrial enterprises, supplying of capital goods, training of Sudanese technicians, and undertaking a geological survey. The Sudanese Government did not accept this offer, taking the position that while it was willing to sell to the U.S.S.R. at auction as much cotton as it wanted to buy, it was opposed to tying such cotton sales to a barter agreement. However, in the following months the Sudan's marketing prospects worsened, due partly to unexpected sales by Egypt of substantial amounts of long-staple cotton to Western European customers, and the Sudanese Government came under increasing domestic pressure to accept the Soviet offer. Late in the year the government marketing board took steps to improve the situation by lowering its prices. This action stimulated sales to the Sudan's traditional customers and enabled the government to continue to delay action on the Soviet offer. Nevertheless, the Sudan is still very vulnerable to this type of approach by the bloc. As of January 1958, more than 200,000 bales of cotton still remained unsold from the 1956–57 crop, and although the 1957–58 crop is expected to be considerably smaller, the world demand for long-staple cotton is weak in relation to shorter-staple cotton; and the Sudan, with attempts at diversification still in the early stages, will continue to be a one-crop economy for some time to come. Under these circumstances, the U.S.S.R. can be expected to continue its attempts to exploit the Sudan's cotton marketing difficulties.

Credits and Technical Assistance. Other bloc activities in the Sudan have been of modest proportions. Since achieving its independence in January 1956, the Sudan has followed a policy of neutrality and has sought to avoid involvements with other powers. Although the bloc has made various offers of technical assistance and arms, the Sudan is not believed to have accepted any bloc credits. The only bloc aid offer accepted by the Sudan was an East German water survey project. East German hydrologists began surveys in early 1956 but, having failed to discover new water resources, abandoned the search in early 1957. Their contract had specified that they were not to receive payment unless water was found. Reports that the Sudan contracted with an East German firm for a complete cotton mill early in 1957 remained unverified.

Bloc countries have made other offers of assistance which the Sudanese apparently have not accepted. Tentative offers of economic assistance were made by the Soviets in 1955, renewed in the spring of 1957, and linked to the Soviets' barter trade offer of August 1957. In 1956 it was reported that the

U.S.S.R. had offered funds for the construction of two dams. Several of the European satellites have offered to assist Sudan by building small factories on very favorable payment terms.

Technicians. The only bloc technicians known to have worked in the Sudan were a handful of East German technicians in connection with the unsuccessful water survey of 1956–57. A Czechoslovak offer to send mechanical and civil engineers and a Soviet offer to supply irrigation and agricultural specialists were not taken up by the Sudanese.

Trade. Sudan's trade is oriented primarily toward the West. Although percentage increases in Sudan's trade with the bloc since 1953 have been significant, exports to the bloc in 1956 were still only $6 million, or just over 3 percent of total exports, while imports were about $7.4 million, or somewhat under 6 percent of total imports. In 1954 exports were about $900,000 and have risen as the European satellites and Communist China increased their purchases of cotton from $700,000 in 1954 to about $5.7 million in 1956. Imports from the bloc have declined since 1954 when they were $11.2 million. In that year the Sudan purchased 75,000 metric tons of sugar from the European satellites. In 1955 sugar purchases dropped to 8,000 metric tons and in 1956 rose to 33,000 metric tons.

In spite of their increased purchases of cotton, bloc countries have not been important purchasers of this commodity thus far, and purchases by the bloc in 1956 amounted to only 6 percent of the Sudan's total sales. The U.S.S.R.'s token purchase of 9,000 bales in the spring of 1957 was its first in recent years and the Soviets have indicated that they do not plan to buy additional cotton unless Sudan accepts its barter agreement offer. In 1956 and 1957 Communist China, the largest buyer among Communist countries, bought 20,000 bales of Sudan's short-staple cotton, about one-half of the annual crop. Short-staple cotton has not encountered the marketing difficulties of long-staple and constitutes less than 20 percent of Sudanese production.

The Sudan has not entered into any trade agreements with bloc countries but in 1955 did sign payments agreements with Czechoslovakia, Poland, Hungary, and East Germany. These agreements apparently facilitated trade with the bloc. The Sudan's 1956 trade with the bloc was 65 percent greater than in 1955.

The bloc has been active in trade promotion and delegations from most bloc countries have visited the Sudan. In early 1956 Heinrich Rau, Deputy Premier and Minister of Foreign Trade of East Germany, and the Sudanese Deputy Prime Minister exchanged visits, and later in the year Czechoslovakia staged an industry exhibit in Khartoum to display agricultural and industrial equipment. In early 1956 a visiting Communist Chinese delegation and the Sudanese Government reached agreement on promoting trade. In late 1957 a Sudanese delegation visited Communist China and the two governments announced agreement on promoting trade, including the exchange of trade missions and the holding of trade missions and the holding of trade exhibitions. The Chinese agreed to "seriously consider" importing Sudanese long-staple cotton and other products "if the quality and price are satisfactory."

Syria[1]

Since 1955 Syria's economic ties with the Sino-Soviet bloc have become progressively closer and stronger. This increase in economic relations is primarily a reflection of political attitudes rather than the result of economic factors. Syria's apprehensiveness concerning Israel and its hostility to "Western imperialism"—stemming from its former colonial status and its belief that the West has promoted and protected Israel—has made it particularly receptive to Soviet-bloc offers of military and economic assistance and expanded trade relations. This anti-Western orientation was intensified significantly by the Anglo-French-Israeli invasion of Suez in late 1956.

Because of the strength of this hostility to the West, economic considerations have been subordinated or ignored despite the objections of the Syrian business community. Syria's important French wheat market was sacrificed by a boycott against shipments to France because of opposition to French policies in North Africa.

In contrast to many other less developed countries that are the target of the Soviet bloc's economic offensive, the Syrian economy is basically sound. With a population of about 4 million Syria is not overpopulated in relation to its potential resources. Agricultural production has increased sharply in recent years, and there is still considerable potential for further expansion. The overall rate of economic growth since World War II has exceeded 4 percent per year, perhaps the highest in the region.

Syria's economic problems are relatively small and fairly manageable compared to many other countries in its stage of development. Nevertheless, there are certain weaknesses in its economy that contribute to its vulnerability to bloc overtures. Its valuable cereals crop is heavily dependent upon climatic conditions; a serious drought can greatly impair its exports of grain. It has also become increasingly dependent on cotton as its major export crop, which has increased its vulnerability to international marketing developments. A minor crop before 1949, 95,000 tons of cotton were produced in 1956; and cotton accounted for 30 percent of the value of all exports that year. Last year Syrian textile manufacturers and wheat producers had difficulty in finding foreign markets.

While the acreage in production can be considerably expanded, agricultural development faces a number of problems. Chief of these are the lack of roads between the Jazirah region of northeast Syria, the granary of the country, and market centers and ports; the lack of storage for the exportable grain surplus; the feudal system of land tenure; lack of credit facilities for small farmers; and the uncertain nature of large-scale agricultural operations.

Syria's close economic ties with the Sino-Soviet bloc are of comparatively recent date. A number of trade agreements with the bloc were signed in 1955, but there was little significant increase in actual trade until late 1956 after the Suez crisis. The first military aid agreement was signed in May 1956, followed by a second in November. Several offers of credits and tech-

[1] This section applies to Syria prior to its incorporation with the United Arab Republic on February 21, 1958.

nical assistance were made by visiting bloc delegations during 1956, but few tangible results in the way of agreements and contracts were apparent until late 1956 and early 1957 when Syria accepted several offers made by Soviet satellites to build industrial installations. Economic collaboration with the U.S.S.R. on a large scale did not begin until the agreement of October 28, 1957, extending up to $168 million in credit to finance the cost of equipment and technicians for 19 major projects. It is still uncertain what effect the political union of Egypt and Syria may have on the implementation of this agreement.

Bloc Credits. The Sino-Soviet bloc had extended $294 million in credits to Syria as of December 31, 1957. Of this amount $194 million is earmarked for economic development and the remainder for the purchase of bloc arms. The Soviet Union has furnished $170 million in credits to cover the costs of bloc equipment and technicians for economic development projects and more than $50 million for arms. Of the European satellites, Czechoslovakia has extended about $50 milllion for arms and $20 million in economic credits. Bulgaria and East Germany have also furnished substantial credits for development projects.

Although Syria received no important credits from the bloc until well into 1956, it is now exceeded only by Yugoslavia, Egypt, and India in the amount of bloc credits accepted. On a per capita basis, it has received by far the most, for its population is relatively small in comparison with other important recipients of bloc aid, such as Egypt, Yugoslavia, India, Indonesia, and even Afghanistan.

In early 1956 Syria and Czechoslovakia reached an agreement on the purchase of arms. The credit extended to cover these purchases is estimated to be about $50 million, and Syria is to service this loan with convertible currency or shipments of cotton, wheat, tobacco, and other commodities.

In November Syria made an agreement to purchase arms from the Soviet Union under a credit. The terms of the credit are not fully known but are believed to be similar to the earlier arms agreement with Czechoslovakia. It is also probable that the visit of Syrian Defense Minister al-'Azm to Moscow in the summer of 1957 resulted in arrangements for additional arms purchases. The bloc is also reported to be assisting in the expansion of military airfields and in the construction of a naval base near Latakia. Toward the end of 1957, Czechoslovakia agreed to postpone payment of the Syrian arms debt from 3 to 7 years. The total Syrian arms purchases thus may come to about $100 million and in addition to their military and political significance, they tend to strengthen Syria's economic ties with the bloc by bringing about a shift in exports from traditional markets to service the credits or by reducing the modest foreign exchange holdings Syria needs for trade with the free world.

A Soviet technical delegation to the Middle East visited Syria in March 1956, followed by a visit by the then Soviet Foreign Minister Shepilov. Shepilov made grandiose offers of aid while there, including the construction of the Yusuf Pasha Dam, the Latakia-Jazirah Railway, grain storage warehouses, airports, etc. In July a second technical mission offered to build grain elevators, flour mills, and other industrial establishments. The East

German Minister of Trade visited Syria in May, and in June a group of Syrian financiers visited the U.S.S.R. in connection with the financing of a proposed Syrian-Soviet Shipping Company. The tangible results of all these missions was limited, however, until the latter part of 1956.

In late 1956 the U.S.S.R. offered to develop the oil resources of northern Syria and to market the output on normal commercial terms; a contract to construct a cement plant in Aleppo was awarded to an East German firm in September 1956; Czechoslovakia obtained contracts for the engineering survey of the Hama cement plant and the construction of two smaller plants; a Bulgarian bid for the construction of grain elevators in northern Syria was accepted in October.

After a long delay, the Czechoslovak organization, Tekhnoeksport, was awarded the contract to construct an oil refinery at Homs with an annual capacity of a million tons. The refinery is to cost $15 million, of which about $10 million will be financed by a long-term credit. Construction is scheduled to take a period of 17 months. Syria granted the U.S.S.R. a contract for the technical supervision of the project in preference to a Western concern. This refinery is the first significant bloc involvement in oil operations in the Middle East, and a successful performance here may facilitate further bloc moves into the petroleum field.

Tekhnoeksport and Skoda are also interested in other potential industrial projects. Skoda is to construct and equip a second sugar refinery near Damascus. Bulgaria has been the second most active of the satellites and equipment and technicians arrived in 1957 under earlier contracts for grain elevators and military barracks at Latakia, the Dumayr Military Base, and a geological survey. Bulgaria also indicated interest in development of projects on the Euphrates River. During the second half of 1957 the Hungarians gained the contract to expand the automatic telephone system of Damascus and to extend service to smaller cities in Syria.

The U.S.S.R. made a major entry in the field of economic assistance in the Middle East when on October 28, 1957, it signed with Syria a large-scale economic agreement that constituted an innovation in the Soviet bloc's economic relations with Middle Eastern states. The agreement represents a formalization of the U.S.S.R.'s August 6, 1957, offer to provide Syria with "large-scale economic and technical assistance."

While the October 28 agreement does not specify the exact amount of the Soviet loan, the Syrian Minister of Economy had stated that it may total $168 million, or 30 percent of the total cost of the Syrian development program, if all projects listed in the agreement are implemented. The text of the agreement, as released, lists 19 different projects—some of them closely related, however—for which the U.S.S.R. will supply assistance. These include the construction of hydroelectric power stations on the Euphrates, Orontes, and Yarmuk Rivers and, in the region of Lake Homs, irrigation projects on the Euphrates, Al Kabir, and Barada Rivers; construction of a railway connecting Aleppo with Latakia and Al Qamishli; construction of bridges across the Euphrates and Khabur Rivers; exploration for petroleum and asbestos and for iron, manganese, and chromium ores, including the preparation of a geological map; construction of thermoelectric power stations in Damascus and Aleppo; establishment of a nitrate fertilizer plant; and development of an agricultural laboratory for scientific research.

While the projects listed in the agreement are apparently based in large part upon previous economic surveys of the country, especially the study conducted by the International Bank for Reconstruction and Development (IBRD) in 1954, they are not in complete accord with the recommendations of the IBRD survey. For example, to meet Syria's transport requirements, the IBRD recommended a network of roads connecting the Jazirah with Aleppo and Latakia, rather than a railway as projected in the current agreement.

According to the October agreement, the Soviet aid will consist of a line of credit in rubles, as well as technical assistance. The ruble credit will be available over a period of 7 years, and is presumably to be coordinated with Syria's 7-year development program. It will be used by Syria to pay for technical services and capital equipment from the bloc. The interest rate has been set at 2.5 percent per year and will be calculated for each part of the credit from the date of its use. The U.S.S.R. will accept repayment either in goods or in convertible currency, to be made in 12 annual installments for each section of the credit, beginning (as amended in December to bring it in closer conformity with the Egyptian credit) after all machinery for a given project has been delivered.

The Syrian refusal of the terms of IBRD's 1955 loan offer was ostensibly based upon the rate of interest demanded by the bank and the alleged infringements upon Syrian sovereignty. The low rates of interest offered by the U.S.S.R. avoids the first of these objections, while article 4 of the agreement is designed to allay Syrian fears respecting its sovereignty. This article stipulates that the Syrian Government will set up the various projects to be implemented under the agreement and will organize all work pertaining to them. The Soviet role purportedly will be limited to supplying technical assistance and necessary capital equipment. However, inasmuch as each project involves a separate agreement to be concluded between Syria and the U.S.S.R., at the appropriate time, there is ample room for the U.S.S.R. to exert controls over the use of the credit. Since the agreement provides that deliveries of capital goods by the U.S.S.R. to Syria will be based upon world market prices, the U.S.S.R. will not be able to charge inflated prices for material supplied under the agreement, and Syria cannot expect to obtain capital goods at giveaway prices.

In Prague, in late December 1957, Syrian and Czechoslovak officials issued a joint communique proposing a technical and economic agreement similar to the Soviet-Syrian agreement. A Czechoslovak mission was to go to Damascus to draw up the details of the agreement.

Despite the magnitude of bloc credit offers accepted by Syria, most projects are still in the survey or initial construction stage and final project agreements have not yet been reached under the $168 million Soviet line of credit. As a consequence, actual bloc performance on projects has not been extensive enough to form definite judgments on its quality.

The first major construction project undertaken by the bloc, the petroleum refinery at Homs being constructed by the Czechoslovaks, ran into some labor difficulties when Syrian workers demonstrated against the practice of hiring workers from the surrounding villages rather than from the Homs labor force and paying these workers at a piece rate equivalent to about 50 percent of the prevailing wage for ordinary workers. At the end of the year, however, initial difficulties were apparently overcome and basic construction work seemed to be proceeding on schedule.

Agreement on 12 contracts under the $168 million Soviet line of credit reportedly was reached by the high level Syrian economic mission to Moscow in December but have not been approved as yet by the Syrian Cabinet. This delay may be connected with the combining of Syria and Egypt into the United Arab Republic at the end of January.

Technical Training. The shortage of technically trained personnel in Syria combined with its dependence on the bloc for arms has furnished the bloc an opportunity to send its technicians there in considerable numbers. Since May 1956 when the first Soviet-bloc arms experts were reported in Syria, the number has increased to where it is now estimated that there are more than 200 military specialists and about 110 other technicians there.

More than half of the military instructors and advisers are from the Soviet Union with most of the remainder from Czechoslovakia and a few from Poland. The greatest number of nonmilitary experts presently in Syria are from Bulgaria, East Germany, and Czechoslovakia. There are yet no Soviet economic technicians there, but they are expected to arrive in number when the first major projects under the Soviet line of credit are begun.

Soviet-bloc military specialists are engaged for the most part in training the Syrian army in assembling and maintaining bloc equipment, but some are assigned to units in the field in advisory capacities.

A few Czechoslovak engineers are now working on the Homs petroleum refinery; but when the intricate machinery is to be installed, 150 Czechoslovak technicians will eventually be employed. Several Bulgarian technicians are working on the contract for a geological survey and more are expected. Other bloc technicians are engaged in the construction of barracks, airfields, cement plants, sugar refineries, and port works. To date there are no indications that the Syrian Government is other than reasonably satisfied with the competence and behavior of these technicians.

Probably several hundred Syrians have gone to various countries of the bloc for military training. Most are undergoing flight training, but some Syrian officers have attended the Military Staff College in Moscow. It is also estimated that about 100 Syrian students have gone to bloc countries to pursue their studies. The great majority of these students are in the European satellites with only a few in the U.S.S.R. and Communist China.

Trade With the Bloc. The Sino-Soviet bloc countries have become important trading partners of Syria only in the very recent past. The bloc's share of Syrian imports was 2.5 percent or $4.8 million in 1954 and rose to only 3.9 percent or $12.7 million in 1956. The bloc took a negligible 0.5 percent or $0.7 million of Syria's exports in 1954, but this rose to 7.8 percent or $11.2 million by 1956. Czechoslovakia led the bloc as a supplier of imports (1.3 percent in 1956), followed by Rumania (0.8 percent) and Hungary (0.5 percent). Czechoslovakia also took the major share of Syria's exports to the bloc in 1955 and 1956 (1.0 and 4.1 percent respectively), followed by Communist China (0.1 and 1.1 percent). Most of the increase in Syria's trade with the bloc in 1956 occurred after the Suez crisis in the latter part of the year. Syria's imports from the bloc consist largely of a variety of manufactured goods, lumber, and petroleum products. Considerable difficulty was experienced with some Soviet products. Automotive equipment was notably unsatisfactory mechanically, and the firm selling this equipment had to close its showrooms despite the fact that the prices on trucks and automobiles were low. Syria's exports to the bloc consist of cotton, wheat, and barley, the chief export crops on which its economic stability largely depends.

During 1957 Syrian trade shifted sharply toward the Soviet bloc. While Western countries still continued to supply most of Syria's import requirements, the Soviet bloc's share of the export market increased substantially. During the first 6 months of 1957 the bloc accounted for 21 percent of Syria's total exports compared with an insignificant portion during the first half of 1956. This sharp increase is largely attributable to the substantial bloc purchases of Syrian cotton.

The role of the Soviet bloc in Syria's trade was probably even larger during the last 6 months of 1957. Bloc countries have reportedly proposed to buy all of Syria's cotton surplus as well as taking substantial quantities of wheat. If these offers are implemented, the Soviet-bloc countries may take as much as 40 percent of Syria's exportable cotton surplus from the 1957 crop. This fundamental reorientation of export trade would almost inevitably result in a marked increase in Syrian imports from the bloc.

In 1955 and 1956 several Sino-Soviet bloc trade missions including one from Communist China visited Syria making attractive trade offers. In October 1956 East Germany opened a consulate in Damascus with a permanent trade representative and a branch of the East German Foreign Trade Bank was opened there. The Soviet Embassy opened a commercial office in the downtown business section, and advertised its goods in the local newspapers offering bargain prices. Earlier, Syrian nationals organized the Syrian Eastern Development Corporation to handle trade with the bloc, undertake the construction of industrial plants, and develop shipping and transportation agencies and other commercial services.

The International Trade Fair at Damascus in September 1956 provided the bloc another opportunity to promote trade ties, and bloc participation was extensive, East Germany, Czechoslovakia, Communist China, and the U.S.S.R. made heavy purchases of space in Syrian newspapers of all political leanings to advertise their exhibits. Participation was also heavy in the 1957 fair. Commercial firms handling bloc goods opened large showrooms in Damascus and Aleppo and prominent businessmen were invited to visit the bloc. East German textile machinery firms quoted generous credit terms that Western suppliers could not meet.

Syria now has trade and payments agreements with the U.S.S.R., all the European satellites, and Communist China. In 1955 when its economic relations started to become increasingly oriented to the bloc, only one such agree-

The Czechoslovak pavilion at the 1956 trade fair at Damascus, Syria.

ment existed. Three trade agreements were negotiated in 1955, four in 1956, and one in 1957. Only India has entered into more trade agreements with the bloc. There is no information available, however, as to the extent these agreements have been fulfilled.

Yemen

In 1955 Yemen had virtually no economic ties with the Sino-Soviet bloc; now, less than 3 years later, Yemen is heavily involved with the bloc. The bloc conducts its economic diplomacy on an opportunistic basis, and in Yemen the border tension with the Aden Protectorate, administered by the United Kingdom, provided occasion for bloc overtures. As a means of strengthening its internal and regional position, Yemen followed the example set by Egypt and accepted arms from the Soviet bloc in 1956.

Another factor which invited bloc overtures was growing pressure in Yemen for modernization and development of the country. The bloc could expect that its offers of aid "with no strings attached" might find a ready acceptance in Yemen which has traditionally favored a policy of neutrality. The United States has also put forward, in response to Yemeni requests, proposals for economic assistance which are currently being considered by the Yemen Government. A number of Western firms have in recent years signed oil concession agreements with Yemen, but so far extensive exploration has not been carried out.

Credits. Yemen is believed to have accepted at least $19 million worth of bloc credits since 1955, $3 million for arms and $16 million for economic assistance.

Lesser credits may have been extended for other projects but available information is not definite.

Arms negotiations had been rumored from the time that Yemen-bloc relations began to expand in 1955. A Soviet delegation which came to Yemen in March 1956 to negotiate a trade agreement reportedly made an offer of arms. Late in 1956 Yemeni officials confirmed reports that Yemen had purchased arms from the U.S.S.R. worth about $9 million. However, Yemen reportedly will have to pay only $3 to $4 million for the equipment, which includes aircraft, artillery, small arms, and ammunition. A number of bloc military technicians have been in Yemen both to supervise assembly of the equipment and to train the Yemenis in its operation.

In the field of economic development and technical assistance, the bloc has undertaken a number of projects since 1955. Some of these are believed to be financed by shipments of Yemeni commodities to the bloc while others may be covered by credits, the value and terms of which are not known. One project involved the improvement of port facilities at Salif. Bloc technicians are also engaged in the development of highways, communications facilities, and light industries. In addition, the U.S.S.R. has completed the renovation of an airport, has sent several planes and pilots to Yemen, and has begun flight training for Yemenis.

In January 1958 Yemen reportedly concluded an agreement with Communist China under which the Chinese are to extend an interest-free loan of about $16 million to finance the construction of roads and light industries in Yemen. Each part of the credit is to be repaid in 10 annual installments following completion of a particular project, with repayment to be in Swiss francs, sterling, or Yemeni commodities. Communist China agreed to send technicians to Yemen and to train Yemeni technicians in Chinese schools.

In addition, bloc countries have made several offers of economic and technical assistance which are not known to have been accepted as yet by the Yemenis. In January 1958 the U.S.S.R. reportedly offered a loan of $25 million at 2.5 percent interest repayable in 15 years, to be used to finance roads, harbor facilities, dams, a survey of mineral resources, and public health facilities. In 1956 the Yemeni Crown Prince stated that the Czechoslovaks had offered well- and canal-digging equipment and a cement factory at prices 30 percent below prevailing world prices. In addition, Czechoslovakia has offered to develop the port of Ras al Kathib.

Technicians. Numbers of bloc military technicians, including military instructors and pilots, are believed to be in Yemen in conjunction with the assembly of bloc military equipment and training in its use. During the last half of 1957, it is estimated that there were about 55 bloc economic technicians in Yemen, including Russians, East Germans, and Czechoslovaks, and there have been recent indications that their numbers may be increasing. These technicians are involved in port construction as well as in the development of highways, communications facilities, and factories. The number of technicians in Yemen has gradually increased during the last 2 years; the Yemenis apparently are satisfied with their performance and deportment.

In addition, technical training for Yemenis is being provided in bloc countries. Yemen has accepted a Czechoslovak offer to train Yemenis in engineering and medicine in Czechoslovakia for a 6-year period free of charge. The U.S.S.R. has agreed to train Yemenis in oil research and mining in Moscow.

Trade. Trade data for Yemen are not available but trade with the bloc is believed to have been negligible before 1956. The bloc offered trade agreements involving imports of bloc technical assistance as an opening gambit when it began to expand relations with Yemen late in 1955. In October of that year, Yemen and the U.S.S.R. signed a treaty of friendship in which both parties agreed to promote mutual trade. In early 1956 a Czechoslovak trade mission visited Yemen to discuss a trade agreement. In March 1956 Yemen and the U.S.S.R. concluded a trade agreement following negotiations which had been in progress since January. The agreement provided for the exchange of Yemeni coffee, dried fruits, and raw hides for industrial equipment, textiles, foodstuffs, and cement. It is likely that the trade agreement was linked to a Soviet offer of technical assistance made at the same time. In July 1956 Yemen signed trade agreements with East Germany and Czechoslovakia which provided for the exchange of Yemeni agricultural products for East German heavy machinery. Beginning in late 1956, Yemeni coffee began moving to the U.S.S.R. and Russian sugar began to arrive in Yemen. Trade agreements were signed in late 1957 with Poland and in early 1958 with Communist China. The latter, in conjunction with an economic aid agreement, provides for the exchange of Yemeni agricultural products for Communist Chinese industrial goods.

Iran

Since the middle of 1956 the Soviet bloc has stepped up its campaign to develop closer economic as well as diplomatic and cultural relations with Iran. During 1955–56 Iran's economic relations with the bloc had been adversely affected by the hostile Soviet reaction to Iran's adherence to the Baghdad Pact. A change in the Soviet attitude became evident after the Shah's visit to Moscow in July 1956. Moreover, after the arrival of the new Soviet Ambassador, Pegov, in Tehran in September 1956, there was a marked increase in Soviet trade offers and proposals for economic and technical assistance. The Government of Iran has agreed to some of these proposals (3-year trade agreement, transit agreement, and border river surveys) which it believes could benefit the Iranian economy without endangering Iranian independence.

Economic and Technical Assistance. Since late 1956 there have been numerous Soviet offers of economic and technical assistance. These have included joint multipurpose development of border river regions, financial as well as technical assistance for a variety of industrial projects, and assistance in improving Iranian ports and internal transport system and in developing petroleum resources in northern Iran. Iran has thus far not accepted any Soviet credit offers. It did, however, reach an agreement with the U.S.S.R. in August 1957 for a joint survey of the multipurpose development potential of the Araxes and Atrek Rivers, which form the border with the U.S.S.R. in northwestern and northeastern Iran respectively. No financial assistance is reportedly involved, and each country will survey its own side of the border.

In addition, discussions are currently being held regarding a similar arrangement for the development of the Hari Rud River on the border of Iran, the U.S.S.R. and Afghanistan.

In October 1957 Iran awarded the U.S.S.R. a contract for completing the construction of one of the four grain elevators begun by the U.S.S.R. prior to World War II. The other three were given to a West German firm. Also in October, Iran reportedly contracted for Soviet services in dredging the Caspian port of Pahlevi but has asked the U.S.S.R. to do the work under the supervision of Kamsax, the Scandinavian syndicate which is surveying Caspian ports. Iran has not yet acted upon the Soviet offer to improve rail facilities between Julfa, on the Soviet border, and Tabriz. Both the dredging of the Caspian ports and the improvement of Iranian rail facilities would facilitate expansion of trade between the two countries.

Trade and Trade Agreements. Trade between Iran and the Soviet bloc rose sharply during 1957 mainly as a result of enhanced Soviet willingness to purchase Iranian commodities and increased Soviet deliveries of goods in settlement of the U.S.S.R.'s World War II debts to Iran. During the first 7 months of 1957, Iran's exports to the bloc were $14 million and imports from the bloc were $21 million, compared with $10 million and $15 million respectively for the same period in 1956. As a share of total trade (excluding oil company transactions), exports to the bloc in 1957 were 25 percent and imports were 12 percent, compared with 17 percent and 10 percent respectively for the first 7 months of 1956 and 18 and 9 percent respectively for all of 1954. However, the bloc share of Iranian trade in 1957 was still far below the percentages taken by the U.S.S.R. and Eastern Europe countries in 1938. The U.S.S.R. usually accounts for 80–90 percent of Iran's exports to the bloc and 65–80 percent of its imports from the bloc. Czechoslovakia, Poland, and Hungary are the only satellites trading with Iran. Principal Iranian commodities exported to the Communist orbit are rice, raisins, wool, cotton, and mineral ores; major imports are sugar, cotton fabrics, iron and steel, and machinery.

During the last year there has been an increase in commercial activity of Soviet trade representatives in Iran. The Soviets have been offering Iranian merchants and industrialists easy credit terms for purchasing Soviet materials and equipment. Moreover, the U.S.S.R. agreed to accept Iranian rice despite the fact that it was not of high quality. Soviet dissatisfaction with Iranian rice had for some time been a minor irritant in commercial relations between the two countries. The Soviet trade delegation recently requested permission from the Iranian Government to hold a trade fair in Tehran for display of Soviet consumer goods and industrial equipment. Also representatives of the Soviet travel agency Intourist have been in Tehran for talks with Iranian officials and travel agencies in order to encourage increased exchange of tourists.

Iran has trade agreements with the U.S.S.R., Czechoslovakia, Hungary, and Poland. Trade with the U.S.S.R. is governed by quotas negotiated annually under the basic Commerce and Navigation Treaty of 1940. Both countries agree to liquidate year end balances by subsequent delivery of goods. In April 1957 a 3-year protocol was signed envisaging annual increases in the level of trade through 1959-60. However, only the 1957–58 quotas were fixed; the 1958–59 and the 1959–60 lists are to be renegotiated. In October 1957 Iran decided to accord the U.S.S.R most-favored-nation customs treatment on a reciprocal basis within the framework of the Soviet-Iranian trade agreement. This will apply only to items which appear both in the Soviet-Iranian trade agreement and the United States–Iranian Reciprocal Trade Agreement. This accord should improve the competitive position of Soviet goods in Iranian markets. Iran's trade agreements with the satellites all have payment provisions which specify swing limits. Balances in excess of these limits are to be liquidated in sterling or other acceptable currency. Levels of trade called for by these trade agreements with the U.S.S.R. and satellites have rarely been realized in recent years.

Because of its geographic location the U.S.S.R. has traditionally been an important trading partner of Iran. Since most of Iran's economic activity outside of oil is carried on in the northern and central parts of the country, transport to the Persian Gulf ports can be costly for many commodities. The U.S.S.R., therefore, is an important outlet for Iranian commodities which cannot be profitably sold to the free world. In recent years Iran has been trying to encourage expansion of its export markets and thus is willing to augment its trade with the Soviet bloc. Any reasonable proposal to improve economic relations with the bloc is therefore given serious consideration. In addition to the 3-year trade protocol and the most-favored-nation arrangement, Iran recently ratified a transit agreement concluded in April 1957 with the U.S.S.R. The accord provides for reciprocal rights of free transit of goods across the U.S.S.R. and Iran to third countries and eliminates certain restrictions in the 1940 transit agreement. Increased use of the transit routes awaits determination of freight rates and improvement of rail facilities in Iran.

Turkey

Turkey's economic relations with the Sino-Soviet bloc began to expand in 1954. Until 1956 this expansion took the form of increased trade. In 1956, this trade declined, but in 1957 Turkish–Soviet bloc postwar economic relations entered a new phase when Turkey accepted medium-term credits from the Soviet Union. The increase in trade since 1954 can be attributed to conditions within Turkey as well as to Soviet-bloc efforts. Inflation in Turkey tended to price its exports out of world markets, and the resulting shortage of foreign exchange forced it to defer credit payments to Western European suppliers. As the shortage of foreign exchange became acute and Turkey's international credit position continued to deteriorate, expanded trade with the bloc became correspondingly more attractive. Credit was available, foreign currencies in short supply were not required, and accounts could be cleared through existing trade and payments agreements. However, diversion of exports from Western to Eastern European markets tended to perpetuate rather than solve Turkey's credit problem in the West, since it increased the difficulty of repaying arrears. In 1955 the Turkish Government decided to slash drastically all imports, including those from the Soviet bloc, and to direct exports toward Western Europe as much as possible. The extreme shortage of imports resulting from this policy has, in turn, made bloc offers of credit and assistance in economic development more attractive.

Bloc Assistance. Turkey has accepted short- and medium-term credits from the Soviet satellites on industrial installations and equipment. In these dealings commercial rather than political motives were predominant on both sides, and on several occasions shipments to Turkey were held up pending payments due on earlier shipments. Imports on credit from the satellites have included motor vehicles, textile machinery, and paper-making machinery.

Prior to 1957 there were frequent Soviet offers of economic assistance. They were grandiose but vague and probably were not taken very seriously by either side. But in April 1957 a change in Soviet policy with respect to Turkey was evident with the arrival in Ankara of a new Soviet Ambassador, Nikita Rijov, an engineer who had worked on Soviet construction projects in Turkey in the 1930's. The new policy was to exert political pressure on Turkey on the one hand and to offer substantial economic assistance on the other. In contrast to earlier offers, those made by Rijov and Soviet commercial delegations visiting Turkey were specific, practical, and attractive. In July 1957 Turkey accepted a 5-year credit for the construction of a flat-glass factory and reached agreement in principle for the Soviet-financed construction of a caustic soda plant. The agreement is significant because it is the first postwar credit of this sort accepted from the U.S.S.R. As in the case of most Soviet credits, this offer was probably based on political considerations. In connection with the agreement it is interesting that glass and caustic soda are two of Turkey's most important imports from the Soviet bloc, and the completion of these plants will tend to reduce rather than increase Turkey's dependence on the bloc. Other recent Soviet offers—not accepted to date—have included credits for the purchase of motor vehicles, aircraft, and textile machinery. Total bloc credits to Turkey under existing agreements approximate $10 million.

A small number of Soviet technicians are expected to supervise the construction of the glass factory, and a few Turks may travel to the U.S.S.R. for training in the operation of the plant. Also, some satellite technicians have been engaged in installing textile and paper-making machinery in Turkey and in training local personnel. Thus far there have been no complaints about the competence of bloc technicians.

Trade With the Bloc. In the case of both exports and imports Turkish trade with the bloc was higher in 1956 than in 1954 but was substantially below the 1955 levels. Thus trade turnover of $100 million with the bloc in 1954 rose to $160 million in 1955 but declined to $119 million in 1956 (exports $60 million, imports $59 million). The bloc share of Turkish foreign trade in this period rose from 12 percent to 20 percent and then dropped to 17 percent. This trend continued during 1957, but the bloc still accounted for 17 percent of Turkish trade in the first 11 months of the year.

Eastern European countries are traditional Turkish markets and sources of supply, and the current share of the bloc in total Turkish foreign trade is only slightly above pre-World War II levels. Turkish trade with the U.S.S.R. approximates the volume of this trade prior to World War II. Turkey's most important bloc trading partners are Czechoslovakia, East Germany, Poland, and the Soviet Union, in that order. Turkey has trade and payments agreements with all these countries and, in addition, with Rumania, Hungary, and Bulgaria. Generally trade falls slightly below agreed quota levels. Turkey's exports to the bloc follow the same pattern as its exports to other areas, except for embargoed items. Agricultural products, especially tobacco, grains, fruits and nuts, and vegetables head the list. Imports from the bloc consist mainly of machinery and transport equipment, iron and steel products, and construction materials. In general, Turkey gets higher prices from the bloc for her exports than she obtains in free-world markets, but she also pays higher prices for imports. This, together with frequent variation in the quality and uniformity in bloc exports, were important factors in the Turkish decision to direct exports toward Western Europe.

The Soviet bloc has not been as energetic in stimulating trade with Turkey as with some other countries, but five bloc countries, including the U.S.S.R., did have exhibits at the 1957 Izmir fair, and a Soviet commercial delegation which visited Turkey at the same time was well received by commercial groups in Istanbul and Izmir. Because of their geographical situation, Anatolia and Eastern Europe are natural trading partners, but it is unlikely in the foreseeable future that trade with the Soviet bloc will approach the volume of Turkey's trade with the West.

VI. AFRICA

The U.S.S.R., now bent on gaining acceptance in Africa as a powerful, respectable, and sympathetic friend, is making increasing use of economic activities to court independent African states. Prior to 1955 the U.S.S.R. showed little interest in Africa and made no efforts, overt at any rate, to influence or to assist the few independent African states. Financial assistance was negligible and was limited to one project in Ethiopia: maintenance support was accorded annually by the U.S.S.R. to the former czarist hospital in Addis Ababa. The Soviet staff at the hospital were the only bloc technicians in Africa. Bloc trade with Africa was nominal and no efforts were made to expand it.

Since the death of Stalin, Soviet policies toward independent African countries have apparently been reassessed, attitudes toward nationalist governments have softened, and since 1955 greater bloc efforts have been made to expand economic relations with Africa. Coincidentally, the emergence of several independent countries, anxious in most cases to demonstrate their independence from colonial powers, has greatly extended the areas in which the bloc can pursue its objectives. Increased attention being given to African studies within the U.S.S.R. and the presence of two Soviet professors on sociological and economic surveys in Ghana in late 1957 indicate growing Soviet interest in the area. The U.S.S.R., free in African eyes from the stigma of colonialism and an example of rapid economic development, has begun in a limited way to take advantage of its opportunities. Efforts, modest to date, have consisted mainly of increasing commercial relations and expanding exchange programs. The U.S.S.R.'s offer of aid made at the Afro-Asian conference at Cairo in December 1957, while mainly a propaganda gesture, may nevertheless herald bloc plans for an augmented economic offensive in the independent countries in the near future.

Bloc Credits and Contracts

There have been no actual contributions of financial aid to African countries, other than the assistance accorded to the small activity in Ethiopia. On the other hand, rumors and reports of liberal Soviet offers of financial assistance have been current since 1955. Such reports have tended to gain circulation at critical periods which strongly suggests that the principal objective was to aggravate relations with the West. For instance, substantial Soviet aid to Libya (a cash or equipment grant, a 20-year loan, and unlimited quantities of wheat) was allegedly offered at the height of negotiations over American assistance in 1956, and another similar offer was made at the time of the 1957 talks. Liberia's President Tubman received an invitation to Moscow to discuss economic aid shortly before Vice President Nixon's visit to Liberia in 1957. The possibility of Czechoslovak and Soviet offers of aid to Tunisia arose during the arms crisis of 1957. The Soviet Union has also allegedly made offers of financial assistance at other times to Tunisia and to Ethiopia. None of these offers, however, has been confirmed or even acknowledged by bloc countries.

In contrast to the nebulous general offers of aid, the bloc countries have participated in international bidding on certain African projects and have made offers (involving credit) to construct others. Czechoslovakia has entered bids on a telephone installation contract in Tunisia, and it has reportedly shown interest in sugar mill, power plant, textile mill, and hospital construction contracts in Ethiopia. Despite several attempts to obtain contracts, the only one awarded to a bloc country (Bulgaria) is for the construction of a $400,000 meat-packing plant in Eritrea, but dissatisfaction has already developed over lack of progress.

Technical Assistance and Exchange Programs

Technical assistance has been of no significance in the bloc economic offensive in Africa to date. The only Soviet technicians known to be in Africa (apart from Egypt and the Sudan) are those at the Soviet hospital in Ethiopia.

While technical assistance is negligible, the exchange-of-persons program sponsored and financed by the bloc has grown considerably in the 2 years since its inception, and may prove to be a most effective method of developing influence and enlisting support for the bloc in Africa. The major emphasis has been directed toward student groups, but representatives of commerce, labor, and cultural activities have been included on many occasions.

In 1957 labor leaders and a National Assembly delegation from Morocco visited Communist China; a Moroccan trade delegation visited Czechoslovakia, the U.S.S.R., and Communist China; a Tunisian women's group went to Communist China; the Liberian Secretary of Commerce and Agriculture attended the Moscow Agricultural Fair; and from 450 to 500 African students from 10 states attended the World Youth Festival in Moscow. In addition to trade teams, a number of bloc delegations traveled to African states during the same period. Morocco was visited by Communist Chinese labor leaders and by touring Chinese students. A Chinese Communist acrobatic group performed in Tunis, and delegates from the U.S.S.R., Hungary, Rumania, and Czechoslovakia attended a student agricultural convention held there. A Chinese Communist cultural delegation was received by Ethiopia. Ghanaian labor leaders have a standing invitation to visit both the Soviet Union and Communist China. During early 1958 Ghana is to send out trade and good will delegations to various countries through the world of which one is to go to the Soviet Union and Czechoslovakia and another to Communist China.

As a concomitant to the expansion of African study programs in the U.S.S.R. and Czechoslovakia, bloc universities have offered scholarships and awards, both general and technical, to African students either directly or through front organizations such as the Communist-controlled International Union of Students. Outstanding examples are the scholarships for 4-year undergraduate training and scholarships for advanced medical and engineering studies which were offered to Ethiopia by the U.S.S.R. and Czechoslovakia. While there are few full-time African students behind the Iron Curtain at present, Communist circles are in contact with many of the Africans studying in the United Kingdom (between 5,000 and 7,000), France (about 6,000), and elsewhere in Europe; and some have been induced to visit bloc countries for short periods of time under various nonstudy programs.

Trade and Trade Relations

The major economic measures currently employed in the advancement of bloc interests in Africa are in the field of trade. Trade between the bloc and independent African states was and remains minor in volume, despite some increases in recent years. African countries have imported machinery, manufactures, automobiles, textiles, and foodstuffs from Bulgaria, Communist China, Czechoslovakia, East Germany, Hungary, Poland, and the U.S.S.R. Czechoslovakia has been the main source of imports, but Moroccan imports of tea from Communist China account for over three-fourths of her bloc imports. Imports from the bloc have shown a higher rate of increase than exports. Most independent African states at least doubled their imports between 1954 and 1956, while Ethiopia increased hers over five-fold. Morocco, Africa's largest importer of bloc goods, obtained only 5 percent of its imports from the bloc in 1956; the bloc accounts for less than 2 percent of the import trade of each of the other African states. Exports to the bloc have remained relatively stable at low levels (less than 2 percent of export trade in all cases), with such notable exceptions as Soviet purchases of Ghanaian cocoa. Exports have also included phosphates from Morocco and Tunisia and coffee from Ethiopia. Ghana and Ethiopia have exported mainly to the U.S.S.R., while Morocco and Tunisia have exported mainly to Bulgaria, Communist China, Czechoslovakia, and Poland.

Two factors which may lead to an increase in bloc trade are (1) the search for additional and, if required, alternative sources of external revenue, as in North Africa; and (2) the desire to escape fluctuating world commodity prices, especially in the case of those countries dependent upon single crops. The association of dependent areas with the European common market may further aggravate the marketing problems of certain independent states which may lead them to seek new markets.

Factors which have heretofore hindered the expansion of bloc trade are the absence of maintenance facilities in Africa for mechanical equipment, the Soviet reputation for poor quality goods, a certain resistance to changes in marketing patterns, and the lack of mutual confidence in fulfillment of contracts. More important than the present volume of trade, however, is the manner in which trade is conducted, both as to negotiation and as to the actual exchange of goods.

The bloc, capitalizing on the desire of the young countries to reduce their commercial dependence on former metropoles, has sent trade delegations to most of independent Africa. These missions, in addition to promoting trade, have developed favorable publicity and have been effective in various other ways in furthering Soviet interests. Several of the African states have declined

A Polish self-propelled grain combine on display at the 1957 international fair at Tunis.

bloc proposals to exchange commercial or diplomatic representatives, but, to some extent, the frequent missions have offset the lack of embassies. Prolonged visits to Morocco have at times amounted to almost permanent missions; and the head of the Czechoslovak trade team that recently negotiated an agreement with Tunisia has been granted a visa to remain in that country for 1 year. The enthusiastic bloc participation in trade fairs, such as those at Casablanca and Tunis and at the Rand Easter Show in the Union of South Africa, are a part of the pattern of winning respect and influence in Africa.

Although trade has been expanded by the efforts of the visiting missions, the only formal bilateral trade and payments agreements negotiated between bloc countries and African states have been with Tunisia, Morocco, and Ethiopia. Both the North African countries have long engaged in trade with the bloc under provisions of various Franco-bloc economic agreements, and the present agreement represents more of a gesture of independence from France than a shift in trading patterns. Both countries continue to trade under French agreements with those Soviet countries with which they have no separate agreements.

Another Soviet tactic has been the manipulation of trade for political ends; bloc purchases motivated by psychological as well as economic considerations have been effective in influencing local opinion. Thus, at the time of Ghana's independence (March 1957), the U.S.S.R. purchased 34,000 tons of Ghanaian cocoa, or 19 percent of Ghana's cocoa exports for the year. During the same period, Ethiopian goatskins and coffee were purchased by the U.S.S.R. at a price well above the depressed world levels; and in the fall of 1957 Communist China bought Uganda cotton valued at $3 million thereby offsetting a marked decline in important Indian purchases.

VII. SOUTHEAST ASIA

Burma

The Sino-Soviet bloc's economic offensive in Burma has consisted mainly of official agreements in the fields of trade and economic aid. However, since about 1950 Communist China has also carried on a less well defined but active campaign to achieve political objectives through the supply of cheap credit to Chinese businessmen in Burma to increase their control over important sectors of Burma's economy.

Two developments provided the opening wedge for the significant bloc economic activities taking place in Burma after 1954. These were (1) the weakening of Burma's marketing position for rice, its major export, and the need to dispose of large rice stocks which had accumulated by the end of 1953; and (2) Burma's desire for both technical and economic assistance to implement its development program. Burma felt forced to seek markets outside of the free world to sell its rice surplus and to accept foreign financial assistance to fill the shortfall in earnings created by the drop in rice prices.

Credits. Bloc assistance to Burma consists of a series of extensive Soviet "gift" projects as well as $12 to 14 million in Sino-Soviet credits. The so-called "gift" projects are barely under way, and final agreements concerning the credits have not yet been concluded. Bloc assistance is to pay for the foreign exchange costs of equipment and services, while Burma will finance local currency costs as well as reimburse the bloc with either "gifts" or repayment in kind. No other firm offers are known to be under consideration; however, press reports have indicated Burma's interest in the acquisition of military equipment from Czechoslovakia.

During the visits to Burma by Khrushchev and Bulganin in late 1955 and by A. L. Mikoyan, First Deputy Chairman of the Council of Ministers of the U.S.S.R., in April 1956, the two countries agreed on a series of projects to be constructed and equipped in Burma by the U.S.S.R. While these were announced as "gifts" from the U.S.S.R., the Burmese Government subsequently announced that it would make a matching gift of equivalent value in rice or other products to the U.S.S.R. The projects consist of a technological institute, hotel, hospital, cultural and sports ensemble, permanent agricultural and industrial exhibition, theater, and conference hall. An implementation agreement was signed on January 17, 1957, and a general contract covering the basic conditions and order of construction on August 30, 1957. The technological institute and hotel in Rangoon and the hospital at Taunggyi are to be started before the end of 1958; all the projects are to be completed by the end of 1963. Payments for the foreign exchange costs of the projects may be made over a

20-year period. On the basis of very rough estimates such costs may be as high as $30 million.

At the end of 1957, Burma and the U.S.S.R. agreed in principle on the extension of two additional loans: a 12-year loan of $4.2 to $6.3 million at 2.5 percent interest to finance the foreign exchange costs of two irrigation projects being planned by a team of agricultural experts from the U.S.S.R. now in Burma, and a 5-year loan of $3.2 million, also at 2.5 percent interest, to construct an agricultural implements factory in Burma.

The three credits from the U.S.S.R. may total as high as $40 million. The loans are for agriculture, which is the mainstay of Burma's economy. The loans for the construction projects are of marginal importance considering the current budget stringency and the need for funds for the development program. However, successful implementation of these projects, most of which are in Rangoon, will be of considerable propaganda value to the U.S.S.R.

At the end of 1957, Burma and Communist China agreed in principle on a loan of $4.2 million at 2.5 percent interest for a textile factory with a capacity of 40,000 spindles. An expansion of textile manufacturing is considered to be an important part of Burma's development program.

Since little progress has been made on the projects to be financed by bloc credits, an evaluation of bloc performance is premature. Of the construction projects, the technological institute is in the most advanced planning stage, and some work has been begun on the preparation of the site. Preliminary surveys have been made of the two irrigation projects in central Burma—at Kyetmauk-taung near Meiktila and on the Thitson stream near Yamethin—for which experts are formulating dam designs and estimating needs for equipment and personnel. Chinese technicians have also made a survey of the site for the new textile factory.

Since about 1950 Communist China has also been trying to penetrate the private sector of Burma's economy through the widespread extension of cheap credit, chiefly through the Rangoon branches of the Bank of China and the Bank of Communications, both controlled by Peiping. Local Chinese borrowers are obliged to comply with Communist directives, e. g., to send their children to Communist schools, fly the Communist flag on appropriate occasions, and participate in the activities of Chinese Communists in Burma. No information is available on the total value of the credit extended.

Technicians and Technical Training. Bloc technicians with a wide range of skills have been visiting Burma since 1956. At present there are at least 60 engaged in work of sufficiently long duration to be considered resident. Of these a minimum of 50 are from the U.S.S.R. and a minimum of 10 from Communist China. Many more are expected in order to implement the "gift" construction projects and the projects planned by the Soviet agricultural team.

In 1956 two Czechoslovak geologists visited Burma, and 7 textile specialists from Communist China arrived to expand the capacity of the Government Spinning and Weaving Factory near Rangoon. This expansion is being done under contracts between the China National Technical Import Corporation and Burma's Industrial Development Corporation signed in July and December 1956. The expenses of the technicians and the equipment for the expansion, now nearly complete, were paid for under Burma's trade agreement with Communist China.

On November 20, 1956, a contract was signed by the Agricultural and Rural Development Corporation of Burma and the All-Union Tekhnopromexport Association of the U.S.S.R. for a 22-man agricultural team which arrived at the end of the year. The contract for this team has now been extended for another year. In addition to planning the two irrigation projects mentioned above, the team has been working on the development of a machine and tractor station and a cooperative village and on various crop improvement experiments. The irrigation loans extended at the end of 1957 will facilitate the expansion of personnel for the agricultural team.

In November 1956 a 30-man Soviet mission consisting of construction engineers for the various projects, economists, and experts in the fields of minerals and petroleum arrived in Burma for preliminary surveys. Since their departure, various Soviet experts have stayed for short periods. About 30 are now in Burma to construct the Technological Institute, and an unknown number are working on other projects. According to press reports, some 200 additional experts from the U.S.S.R. may be expected in the near future to implement the construction projects.

In 1957 a Polish mining expert arrived to advise on the development of zinc deposits under the auspices of the United Nations Technical Assistance Program. The Polish Prime Minister, in Burma on a trade promotion visit, presented Burma with a medical laboratory. Four Soviet scientists spent a brief period in Rangoon to present equipment for four laboratories and books to the University of Rangoon. They also assembled the laboratory equipment and lectured on its use.

In October 1957 additional textile experts from Communist China arrived to train Burmese workmen in handling Chinese machinery at the Government Spinning and Weaving Factory. The entire group will probably be used to build the new textile mill for which Communist China has just extended a $4.2 million credit.

Although the bloc countries have trained Burmese nationals in Burma, few have received instruction outside the country. In 1957 there were four Burmese students in the U.S.S.R. on Soviet Government scholarships. These scholarships are awarded for a 3- to 4-year period, of which the first year is devoted to learning the Russian language. The Government of Burma chooses the fields of the scholarships, usually in scientific or engineering subjects.

Trade. Burma's trade with the bloc reached a peak in 1956 as a result of Burma's earlier agreements with bloc countries to dispose of its rice stocks and the need to utilize growing credit balances. Exports to the bloc were valued at $39.2 million [1] and imports at $37.5 million, or 17.4 percent of Burma's total world trade. This compared with exports of $43.1 million and imports of $4.1 million in 1955 (11.6 percent of total world trade) and exports of $0.1 million and imports of $3 million in 1954 (less than 1 percent of total world trade). Trade with the bloc would presumably have been even higher in 1956 if cash customers for rice had not been available and if bloc countries, particu-

[1] Including exports of $4.5 million to North Viet-Nam.

larly the U.S.S.R., had provided Burma needed imports at satisfactory market prices. Burma curtailed its trade with the bloc in 1957, chiefly through a reduction in rice shipments. From January to June 1957 exports amounted to $13 million and imports to $14.8 million, 10.6 percent of Burma's total world trade. In all 3 years Communist China and the U.S.S.R. were Burma's principal bloc customers and Communist China and Czechoslovakia the main source of bloc imports. Capital goods, including transportation equipment, were furnished chiefly by Czechoslovakia, East Germany, and the U.S.S.R. and consumers goods, mainly textiles, by Communist China. Burmese shipments to bloc countries have been almost entirely of rice, although some rubber and raw cotton have been shipped to Communist China and lumber to East Germany.

All of the bloc countries have tried to stimulate Burmese purchases by extensive advertising in the press. Communist China held a large economic exhibition in Rangoon from March 20 through April 9, 1957, which was well attended. Visits of bloc officials have been used to encourage Burma to negotiate trade agreements and to stimulate trade.

Beginning in 1954 Burma negotiated a series of trade and payments agreements with the bloc to dispose of its surplus rice. A protocol to the trade agreement usually placed payments on a clearing account basis and specified the volume of rice shipments. In most cases, balanced trade was envisaged. When all were in force in 1956, the agreements called for rice shipments to the bloc of approximately 750,000 tons, or 35 to 40 percent of Burma's annual rice export. Actual shipments, however, were short of this level (nearly 400,000 tons in 1955 and nearly 300,000 tons in 1956).

By 1957 the market for rice was so improved that Burma moved to put its rice trade on a cash basis and disengage itself from its commitments. It did this by terminating the agreements, reducing the quantities of rice involved, or allowing the protocols to lapse. Sizable net credits, mostly with the U.S.S.R., in its clearing accounts with bloc countries which were difficult to utilize were added reasons for this change in policy. In 1957 Burma's agreements with Communist China and Poland were terminated. Agreements are currently in force with seven countries: trade agreements with Bulgaria, Rumania, and North Korea (for these countries, all payments are made on a cash basis and no clearing account is maintained), and trade and payments agreements with Czechoslovakia, East Germany, Hungary, and the U.S.S.R.[2] Only the agreement with the U.S.S.R. contains an annual rice commitment, which was drastically reduced in 1957.

Burma has encountered difficulties in some of its trade deals on a barter basis. These included delays in obtaining merchandise, failure to meet specifications, the delivery of goods in damaged condition, and in some cases extreme overpricing. Hungarian prices were sometimes as much as 50 percent above pre-agreement quotations, and those of other bloc countries were reported to have been similarly adjusted after Burma had committed itself through the barter deals. Burma, undoubtedly, desires that trade be on a cash basis and is mov-

[2] The agreements with Czechoslovakia and East Germany were to terminate on January 31, 1958. No information is available as to their present status. A new trade agreement with Communist China was concluded on February 21, 1958. Details are not yet available but trade will probably be on a cash basis with no trade goals set.

ing toward complete elimination of the clearing account arrangements. Prime Minister U Nu has publicly declared that "a man who takes barter when he can get cash must be out of his mind." On the other hand, Burma is committed to exchanging its rice for technical and financial assistance as evidenced most recently in the loans from Communist China and the U.S.S.R.

Cambodia

The Kingdom of Cambodia, occupying the southwestern portion of what was formerly French Indochina, is bordered by Thailand, Laos, and Viet-Nam. Its location is particularly strategic in terms of possible Chinese Communist aggression into Southeast Asia. Cambodia has a population of about 4 million, the great majority of whom are engaged in agriculture. Rice is by far the chief crop, although rubber, sugar, kapok, and tobacco are also grown. Like most less developed countries, Cambodia earnestly desires economic development and has received considerable aid and technical assistance from France and the United States. The major French project is the development of a seaport at Kompong Som which will enable Cambodia to have a seaport of its own, thereby reducing its dependence on the Vietnamese port of Saïgon. American aid has been devoted to the construction of a highway providing access to the port as well as to a variety of agricultural and social development projects.

Cambodia has espoused a policy of neutralism, a policy of "balancing" relations between the two power blocs. This policy has heightened Cambodia's interest in obtaining economic aid from the Sino-Soviet bloc, primarily Communist China. Cambodian leaders have argued that their national independence is strengthened if foreign assistance is obtained from several sources, thereby avoiding exclusive dependence on one benefactor.

Responding to an invitation made at the Bandung Conference by Communist Chinese Premier Chou En-lai, Prince Sihanouk, then Premier, visited Communist China in February 1956. He was honored by banquets given not only by Chou but by the very inaccessible Chinese Communist Party Chairman, Mao Tse-tung. A rally attended by 8,000 people reportedly was staged. The Chinese Red Cross produced a gift of about $34,000 for the relief of victims of a Phnom Penh fire. Although the resulting joint communique was couched in general, noncommittal terms, Prince Sihanouk was reported by the Communist press to have stated at a Peiping press conference that the time was ripe for Cambodia to cooperate with the Chinese in the economic and cultural fields. An invitation to visit Cambodia was extended to Chou En-lai. On April 4, 1956, a Cambodian trade delegation departed for Peiping. The delegation was headed by Huot Sam Ath, who had primary responsibility for economic planning. Reporting the departure, the American Ambassador in Phnom Penh on April 6, 1956, commented: "Current prospects are without a doubt for a deeper economic penetration by the Communist bloc into Cambodia."

Bloc Assistance. On April 24, 1956, a trade and payments agreement was signed in Peiping and an aid agreement was drafted. On June 21, following 2 weeks of negotiations, the representatives of Cambodia and Communist China signed an aid agreement in Peiping. Communist China agreed to extend a grant of "800 million riels, equivalent to 8 million pounds sterling" which in turn is equal to $22.4 million, for a 2- or possibly 3-year period. Chinese technicians and specialists were to be provided. June 21, 1956, marks Communist China's first venture into the aid sphere of the economic offensive.

The joint communique set forth a host of projects: "construction of textile mills, cement, paper, and plywood factories, establishment of farm irrigation, providing rural centers with electricity, the construction of universities, hospitals, youth and sport centers, roads, bridges, and so forth." The communique went on to state: "The aid from China is not subject to any condition. . . . The Chinese Government will not interfere or exercise any control." *People's Daily*, the Chinese Communist equivalent of *Pravda*, editorialized on June 23: "Asian nations fighting to achieve or strengthen their national independence realize that in order to be free forever from colonialist oppression, poverty and backwardness, they must expand their national economy and carry out industrialization. The imperialist powers were trying desperately to prevent the backward countries from carrying out economic development and industrialization. From the point of view of content, terms and results especially, the economic 'aid' given the underdeveloped countries by the imperialist powers has always violated the sovereignty and interests of the receiving countries and impaired the independent growth of their national economy."

The Communist Chinese obligated themselves to furnish only goods, not foreign exchange. A kind of counterpart fund was to be created by the sale on the Cambodian market of Chinese merchandise. The fund would be used to pay, among other things, "the remuneration of the technicians and the specialists provided by China, as well as the expenses of all natures engaged by them on the territory of Cambodia." The agreement also provided for a Communist Chinese economic mission in Phnom Penh, the chief and deputy chief of which were to be accorded diplomatic privileges. This provision was particularly interesting in view of Cambodia's nonrecognition of the Peiping regime.

Communist China is not the only bloc country which had made aid overtures to Cambodia. The Soviet Union dispatched a 16-member economic mission to Phnom Penh in November 1956 which remained there for several months. Other than an agreement to assist in the construction of a 500-bed hospital, however, no general aid agreement was concluded, apparently because the U.S.S.R. was unwilling to meet Cambodia's request that any aid be provided on a grant basis. Premier Cyrankiewicz of Poland visited Cambodia in March 1957, returning Prince Sihanouk's visit to Warsaw in June 1956, and expressed Poland's readiness to provide specialists in all fields to help Cambodia in its economic development, but, again, no aid pact resulted. Czechoslovakia reportedly offered "whatever scientific and technical aid Cambodia may consider to be important for the development of her economy."

On September 21, 1956, an 11-member Communist Chinese economic mission, including four technicians, finally arrived in Phnom Penh. Eight additional technicians arrived on November 29 to conduct surveys in connection with the four factories to be constructed. In November Chou En-lai visited Cambodia. The first shipment of aid goods, however, did not arrive until April 30, 1957, 10 months after the signature of the aid agreement.

The first shipment consisted of cement and raw silk. Additional shipments gradually arrived and by mid-June the first allocation of counterpart funds was decided upon. Local currency amounting to about $1.5 million was divided between irrigation projects and social welfare projects. By mid-October a number of irrigation ditches and canals had been dug and various livestock and agricultural projects were under way. By the end of the year over $5 million of aid goods had arrived. In addition to the aforementioned cement and silk, the goods received included iron and steel products, cotton thread and fabrics, and paper and silver bullion. It was decided that $14 million of the aid will be devoted to the construction of cement, paper, textile, and plywood factories, in that order of priority. It was apparent from an official announcement dated December 18 that actual construction was still a long way off. Further studies on the cement plant were to be made by Communist Chinese experts; an additional 6 months was required for the completion of construction plans for the textile plant; and perhaps a year would be required for the completion of the plans for the plywood and paper mills.

Technical Training. In September 1957 two Cambodians left for Communist China to receive training in radio operations in connection with the announced gift of a radio transmitter to Cambodia. This is the only known instance in which Cambodians have been sent to the bloc for technical training. A technical cooperation agreement with Czechoslovakia was signed on October 6, 1956, but does not appear to have been implemented in any way.

Trade With the Bloc. Except for imports from Communist China, primarily under the aid program, the Kingdom's trade with the bloc has been negligible. Trade promotion activities by the bloc included Communist Chinese participation in several trade fairs and visits by Czechoslovak, Polish, Soviet, and North Vietnamese trade missions.

The trade agreement with Communist China, signed on April 24, 1956, provided for $14 million of trade each way. Detailed lists of goods which might be traded were published, actual trade appears to have been negligible in the first year of its operation. Trade and payments agreements were concluded with Czechoslovakia on October 6, 1956, with the Soviet Union on May 31, 1957, and with Poland on December 17, 1957. It was not until September 1957 that lists of commodities which might be traded with Czechoslovakia were published. These lists specified trade valued at $350,000. Two months later, similar lists governing trade with the U.S.S.R. were published, valued at $700,000. These lists do not include rubber, Cambodia's largest earner of hard currency, but specify Cambodian rice and extractive products as exports and various types of manufactured goods as imports. Recently North Viet-Nam has energetically sought to establish trade relations with Cambodia. The visit of a North Viet-Nam delegation resulted in a joint communique dated October 31, 1957, which stated that "the delegations recommend to their Governments that a trade agreement be negotiated." Immediately thereafter, a second North Viet-Nam delegation made an appearance at the Phnom Penh Industrial Exhibition.

Although little enthusiasm has been noted within the Cambodian business community for trade with the Communist countries, the Sino-Soviet bloc has maneuvered itself into a position which could facilitate trade, particularly if difficulties arise in the important Franco-Cambodian trade.

Indonesia

Indonesia is by far the largest and most populous country in Southeast Asia. Its long island chain extends from the southeast tip of the Asian mainland eastward to New Guinea and Australia and lies astride major world trade routes. Its resources yield important strategic materials, including rubber, tin, and petroleum, and are capable of significant further development. Because of its size and potential importance, and because critical internal problems have created a favorable climate, Indonesia has become a major Asian target of the Communist-bloc economic offensive.

Formal trade relations were established with the Soviet bloc while Indonesia still was under Netherlands administration. These arrangements were retained by the Indonesian Government after independence in 1949; however, the volume of trade was insignificant. Beginning in 1953 a marked expansion in economic relations with the bloc took place; thereafter new trade and payments agreements were signed, trade, while still insignificant, increased, and Indonesia also accepted bloc credits.

This expansion coincided with the beginning of the Communist bloc's worldwide economic offensive. Declining export earnings in traditional Western markets following the end of the Korean hostilities provided Indonesia with the economic impulse to seek alternative export outlets.

In the last months of 1957 Indonesia was confronted with economic dislocations resulting from the loss of central government control over certain areas of the country and from the seizure of Dutch economic interests. It was against this background of rapidly deteriorating economic conditions that the bloc's largest aid offer—a $100 million development credit from the U.S.S.R.—was finally approved by the Indonesian Parliament in February 1958.

Credits. Bloc economic credits accepted by Indonesia to date total $109 million. In addition the Chinese Communists allowed Indonesia 3 years to settle a trade balance of $16 million, and several thousand military vehicles are being purchased from the U.S.S.R. under a 5-year credit. Various other offers of economic and military aid have recently been made by bloc countries; however, a proffered $20 million credit for light industry from Communist China is the only offer now pending for which a definite value has been announced. No significant grant aid has been offered Indonesia by the bloc.

The largest bloc offer of aid is the $100 million credit for economic development from the U.S.S.R. Although the U.S.S.R. aid agreement was signed in September 1956, Indonesian approval was delayed for almost 18 months. The Indonesian Parliament finally passed the bill authorizing ratification of the arrangement early in February 1958. When urging parliamentary approval of the agreement, government spokesmen in Djakarta cited its similarity to an earlier credit from the United States, also for $100 million, extended by the Export-Import Bank.

The agreement provides that the U.S.S.R. will undertake surveys of Indonesian resources (specifically mentioned were minerals and building materials) and transportation facilities, will plan and assist in the establishment of industries, and will provide training for Indonesian technicians. In addition to these technical services, the U.S.S.R. will supply machinery, equipment, and construction materials for industrial projects. The agreement furthermore calls for Indonesian-Soviet cooperation in the peaceful uses of atomic energy, the U.S.S.R. to provide technical services and training facilities in this field.

Implementation of the basic agreement is contingent on Indonesian requests for specific services or materials and on the negotiation of separate contracts to cover each project. The $100 million credit is to be used for the proposed resource surveys, industrial equipment, and imported building materials. Other expenses are to be defrayed by Indonesia in local currency. Repayment of credits used under the basic agreement is to be made by Indonesia within 12 years at an interest rate of 2.5 percent. Repayment may be effected in Indonesian goods, in transferable pounds sterling, or in a freely convertible currency, subject to agreement between the two governments. According to government spokesmen in Djakarta, the order of specific projects to be undertaken with the Soviet credit has not yet been determined.

An arrangement for deferred payment of current imports was obtained by Indonesia in its revised trade agreement of November 1956 with Communist China, by which Indonesia's accumulated trade deficit was funded, the outstanding balance of about $16 million to be settled within 3 years by shipment of Indonesian goods to Communist China.

Indonesia has accepted a credit of $7.4 million from East Germany for the construction under East German supervision of an integrated sugar refinery. Repayment is to be made within 6 years at 4 percent interest and may be in the form of Indonesian exports.

Approximately $1.5 million has been earmarked under the terms of an open-end credit agreement concluded with Czechoslovakia in May 1956 for the construction of a tire and rubber goods factory. As in the case of the East German operation, the Czechoslovak credit evidently is for 5 to 6 years at 4 percent, and payments may in effect be in the form of Indonesian exports, subject to approval of Czechoslovakia.

Early in 1957 Indonesia ordered approximately 4,000 jeeps and certain other military vehicles from the U.S.S.R. under a 5-year credit. Details of the arrangement were not announced; however, about 1,600 Soviet vehicles reportedly have been received to date.

The only outstanding bloc credit offer reported in specific amount is a proposed Communist Chinese credit for economic development—primarily of the textile industry—in the amount of $20 million. This offer, first made probably in the latter part of 1957, has not yet been definitely accepted.

Indonesia's growing political and economic difficulties, particularly those arising from regional dissidence and the seizure of Dutch interests late in 1957, have attracted intensified Communist interest; and a number of additional

A sugar plant under construction by East Germans at Jogjakarta, Indonesia.

offers of credit assistance from bloc countries have been reported in the past 2 months. The U.S.S.R. and Poland are reported to have made offers of ships to replace the Dutch-operated line which formerly served the vital interisland trade, and the Indonesian Government has agreed to purchase from the U.S.S.R. 10 small intercoastal ships totaling 23,000 tons under the $100 million Soviet loan agreement. The Soviet bloc has also indicated its preparedness to meet the needs of the Indonesian military establishment. Indonesian military purchasing missions traveled to Europe in January 1958 and made purchases in Czechoslovakia and Poland.

Details of the more recent bloc offers of ships and arms are lacking; however, in view of Indonesia's depleted finances, any substantial acquisitions most probably would entail credit arrangements.

The two development projects undertaken in Indonesia with bloc financial and technical assistance—the sugar refinery financed by East Germany and the tire factory financed by Czechoslovakia—were initially welcomed by the Indonesian Government as substantial contributions to the economy. However, the projects have encountered problems, and progress on both is far behind schedule. The sugar factory was originally to be completed in 1956 and still is not in operation; similarly, the arrival of Czechoslovak equipment for the tire factory was delayed by from 3 to 6 months. To date the two bloc undertakings have suffered by comparison with a United States-sponsored cement factory project in Java which was completed ahead of schedule and to the evident satisfaction of the Indonesians. There has been a marked lack of Indonesian comment, either by officials or in the local press, on the two bloc projects in the past year.

The acquisition of Soviet jeeps in 1957 was the occasion for spirited, but inconclusive, press comments regarding quality and price compared with similar United States vehicles. Leftist papers maintained that the Soviet jeeps had been found satisfactory after thorough testing by the Indonesian armed forces, and that their greater capacity combined with the convenient payment terms offered by the U.S.S.R. outweighed any alleged price advantage held by the U.S. product. The U.S.S.R. jeeps already delivered reportedly have been distributed to various military units in Indonesia.

Technical Training. The number of Sino-Soviet bloc technicians in Indonesia has grown progressively to around 100 by the beginning of 1958. While some bloc technical experts in earlier years were reported to have made brief investigations of certain mineral deposits and irrigation projects, most of the foreign Communist technicians currently in Indonesia are assigned to the two bloc construction projects. The sugar factory project is reportedly staffed by about 75 East Germans and at least 20 Czechoslovaks are working on installation of the tire factory. A few Soviet technicians also were sent to Indonesia to train local personnel in the operation and maintenance of the U.S.S.R. jeeps. About eight Soviet nationals were reported to have arrived in mid-1957 for this work.

The conduct of bloc technicians in Indonesia has not been the subject of extensive public comment. Evidently they are competent and have avoided extracurricular contact with Indonesians. Recent parliament debates on the $100 million Soviet economic program, however, revealed widespread uneasiness over the prospective presence of large numbers of bloc nationals in the country. Remarks by some members of parliament reflected concern over the possible subversive potential of a large corps of foreign Communist technicians in Indonesia as well as over the detailed knowledge of Indonesia's resources which would become available to the Communist countries from the proposed surveys.

Offers of additional technical assistance have been made by most bloc countries to Indonesia, and Communist spokesmen have been particularly vocal on this theme since the Indonesian take-over of Dutch enterprises and the consequent departure of many Dutch technicians. East Germany, for example, has made blanket offers to supply technical experts in a wide range of activities, including airline pilots and merchant marine officers. In a recent state visit to Indonesia, Czechoslovak Premier Siroky offered technical cooperation. The Hungarians have indicated a readiness to supply industrial experts. However, most of these offers were made in general terms, and it is unlikely that there have been serious negotiations on specific technical aid projects with these countries. The U.S.S.R. economic development agreement contains the major tangible prospect of additional bloc technical assistance, and, as noted above, it is this element of the agreement which drew substantial criticism in the Indonesian Parliament. The actual number and categories of technicians to be provided by the U.S.S.R. under the agreement are not specified, but the nature of projects proposed implies the use of substantial numbers.

For several years Indonesians have been receiving technical and general academic training in Sino-Soviet bloc countries. The facilities offered evidently include in many cases substantial financial assistance to trainees and students with courses ranging from engineering to music. The scarcity of advanced educational facilities in Indonesia and the growing demand for technical and professional skills undoubtedly are major factors in the acceptance of training opportunities abroad wherever offered. Although probably small in relation to the large number of Indonesian students in Western institutions, the number of Indonesians studying in bloc countries now exceeds 100. East Germany has offered to make room in its educational institutions for Indonesian students leaving the Netherlands.

Trade. Indonesia's trade with the Sino-Soviet bloc increased rapidly after 1953; it reached a peak of $74 million in 1955, registering a threefold increase over the previous year. However, trade with the Communist bloc still is relatively insignificant; the 1955 record represented but about 5 percent of Indonesia's total foreign trade. Exchanges with the bloc dropped in 1956 to $68 million (about 4 percent of total trade), but recorded shipments to and from the bloc in the first 6 months of 1957 amounted to $45 million, indicating resumption of the upward trend.

In earlier years the European satellites, particularly Czechoslovakia and Hungary, were Indonesia's major bloc trading partners; however, since 1955 Communist China has surged to the fore, accounting in 1956 for over 60 percent, and in the first half of 1957 for about 86 percent, of total Indonesian trade with the bloc. The rise in trade with Communist China during the first 6 months of 1957 was attributable almost entirely to a sharp increase in Indonesian exports, which reversed the previous deficit pattern; in this period exports exceeded imports from Communist China by about $3 million. The implication is that Indonesia was making progress in reducing its accumulated trade deficit in accordance with the November 1956 agreement mentioned above.

Textiles account for the bulk of imports from Communist China; exports formerly comprised copra, sugar, rubber, hard fibers and other products, but more recently they have consisted primarily of rubber. In the first half of 1957, 36,000 tons of rubber were exported to Communist China, accounting, by value, for over 90 percent of all exports to that country. Exports to Soviet-bloc countries in Europe also are confined almost entirely to rubber, the U.S.S.R. and Poland being the major customers; the two main imports from the European bloc were textiles and machinery, with the remainder comprising a wide variety of manufactured articles. The Sino-Soviet bloc has not as yet become either a major supplier or a major purchaser of any significant Indonesian trade item. Bloc trade promotion efforts in Indonesia, however, have been widespread and intensive. Most bloc countries now have official trade representatives in the capital, Djakarta, some having been sent before diplomatic relations were established with Indonesia. Bloc trade representatives also have been installed at other major Indonesian commercial centers, including Medan and Surabaya. Commercial agents have been appointed in Indonesia for some bloc trading enterprises and bloc products are advertised effectively. These standard procedures have been reinforced by numerous visits of bloc trade delegations to Indonesia and by the efforts of high level official visitors, the most recent being Czechoslovak Premier Siroky, who frequently concern themselves with trade relations.

In general, the bloc appears to have been alert to trade opportunities in Indonesia and has attained some success in penetrating the Indonesian market with cotton textiles, machinery, iron and steel products, and various types of consumer soft goods. Bloc efforts in this direction will be facilitated by the elimination of Dutch predominance in Indonesia's foreign trade.

Indonesia has trade and payments agreements in force with all Communist-bloc countries except Albania, Bulgaria, and North Korea; in addition, an unofficial trading arrangement is in effect with the last named area. While the earlier versions of Indonesia's agreements with the Communist states provided for quotas, bilateral barter transactions, and inconvertible clearing accounts, these provisions subsequently were found by the Indonesians to be undesirable, since in some instances Indonesia in effect was providing short-term, interest-free financing—which it could ill afford—for bloc trade deficits, particularly for some of the European satellites. Consequently, the agreements were renegotiated to exclude such provisions; trade with the bloc now generally is permissive and shipments are payable in convertible currencies on a current basis. The only exception to the rule is the arrangement with Communist China, owing undoubtedly to Indonesia's large accumulated trade deficit. In this case, the annual trade quotas were increased in 1956 (from $8.4 million to $33.6 million), the clearing arrangement was retained, and Indonesia was given 3 years to work off its trade deficit in goods.

Although disillusioned with the operation of the earlier bloc trade and payments agreements and more aware of limitations in bloc trade, Indonesia's attitude toward expanded commerce with the Communist countries is generally favorable. Nevertheless, it is noteworthy that in the administration of trade and exchange controls no sustained preference has been accorded to bloc commerce. Indonesia evidently is not willing as yet to forcefully divert its trade to the bloc purely out of political considerations. The virtual rupture of economic relations with the Netherlands in recent months will probably disrupt traditional Indonesian trade patterns to a marked degree, since a substantial portion of Indonesia's trade flowed through Netherlands entrepot and marketing facilities and even more of it was handled by Dutch trading and financial houses in Indonesia. Alternative channels now being explored involve mainly free-world countries, notably West Germany; however, the attending dislocations unquestionably afford opportunities for bloc exploitation. The developing shortage of imported goods in Indonesia will lessen buyer discrimination, while extreme foreign exchange stringencies will augment Indonesia's receptivity to credit arrangements whatever the source.

VIII. SOUTH ASIA

Afghanistan

Both the U.S.S.R. and Czechoslovakia early showed an interest in extending economic and technical assistance to Afghanistan by concluding agreements with that country in 1954. Under continuing programs, the amount of Soviet economic aid extended now amounts to at least $121 million, although less than half of that amount would appear to have been obligated. In addition, the U.S.S.R. has provided arms for modernization of the Afghan armed forces. Total aid from the Sino-Soviet bloc amounts to about $161 million.

Soviet economic aid has been concentrated in the fields of transportation, irrigation, and power, while Czechoslovak assistance has gone to light industry. The projects have generally fitted into the Afghan program for economic development. Although negotiation of agreements has been rapid, there have been long lags between initial surveys and actual construction, with the result that very few of the projects sponsored by the bloc have been completed. The credits are uniformly repayable in Afghan commodities. The only grants received have been 15 buses and some hospital equipment from the U.S.S.R., plus a few Soviet taxis.

The first Soviet agreement to supply economic and technical assistance to Afghanistan was signed on January 27, 1954, providing a credit of $3.5 million for the following projects: (1) two silos for the storage of wheat with a capacity of 20,000 tons each, one in Kabul, and the other in Pul-i-Khumri; (2) a flour mill in Kabul with a daily capacity of 10 tons of fine flour and 50 tons of ordinary flour; and (3) a bakery in Kabul with a capacity of 50 tons of flour per day designed to supply the bread requirements of about 50,000 persons, one-third of Kabul's population. All of these projects were completed by mid-1957; the credit, bearing a 3 percent interest charge, is repayable in 5 years, commencing in 1957.

Final approval was announced in February 1955 of a Soviet loan of $2.1 million for highway and paving projects. This credit was used to construct two asphalt factories, of which one in Kabul has been completed, and to pave about 40 kilometers of Kabul's streets, a project which has also been completed as far as Soviet assistance is concerned.

During the visit of Bulganin and Khrushchev in December 1955, the Soviet leaders offered 15 busses and equipment for a 100-bed hospital in Kabul. This gift was delivered on March 28, 1956.

At the conclusion of their visit, it was announced that the U.S.S.R. had agreed to furnish Afghanistan with a $100 million credit for projects upon which separate contracts would be signed later. No repayment would be required for the first 8 years, after which it would be repayable over 22 years at a 2 percent interest rate. On March 1, 1956, a supplementary agreement specified that the following projects would be covered by the loan: (1) two hydroelectric plants of which one at Naghlu is to have a 60,000 kilowatt capacity and the other at Pul-i-Khumri a 9,000 kilowatt capacity; (2) three workshops for the maintenance of motor vehicles at Kabul, Pul-i-Khumri, and Herat; (3) a laboratory for testing materials; (4) a highway through the Salang Pass of the Hindu Kush mountain range; (5) four irrigation projects at Kharwar, Sardeh, Paltu, and Jalalabad (Barikao); and (6) the reconstruction of the airport at Kabul and the construction of an air terminal at Bagrami. In announcing Afghan ratification of the loan agreement on August 16, 1956, Moscow radio mentioned that surveying had commenced on a nitrate fertilizer plant, a project which is probably covered by the agreement of March 1, 1956. The provision of a mobile road maintenance unit, the construction of four more oil depots, an additional hydroelectric and irrigation project, and improvement of the harbor at Qizil Qala all may have been added later to the list of projects covered by the $100 million loan. Although preliminary surveys have been made by Soviet technicians on these projects under the $100 million loan, actual construction has been initiated only on one or two.

On July 30, 1957, at the conclusion of a visit of King Zahir Shah to the Soviet Union, a communique announced that the U.S.S.R. had offered to provide technical and economic assistance in prospecting for oil in northern Afghanistan and to train Afghan technicians, that the two countries would cooperate in exploiting frontier waterways, and that at some future date a treaty on administration of the frontier would be concluded. An agreement for oil exploration was signed in January 1958 and is reported to involve an additional $15 million credit.

On September 2, 1957, Afghan Foreign Minister Naim announced that Afghanistan would receive military aid under an agreement with the U.S.S.R. concluded in 1956. He said that Afghanistan had signed the agreement because it could not obtain arms from other countries on favorable terms. It is believed that this aid amounts to $25 million and that most of these arms have arrived.

Czechoslovakia entered the field of economic and technical assistance to Afghanistan through an agreement signed on August 22, 1954, which provided a credit of $5 million with repayment to commence 3 years thereafter. Under this agreement, a cement plant with an annual capacity of 30,000 tons has been constructed at Jabal-us-Seraj and a survey completed on a second cement plant at Pul-i-Khumri, which is to have an initial capacity of 200 tons daily and an eventual capacity of twice that amount. Preliminary surveys have been made for a fruit conservation plant at Kandahār with a capacity of 30,000 tons per year and for a brick kiln and roof tile factory near Kabul. Additional Czechoslovak projects on which preliminary surveys have been completed are tanneries at Kabul and Herat, a shoe factory at Kabul, and a city water system for Mazar-i-Sharif.

The only other source of economic assistance has been Poland, which offered to install new machinery and renovate two woolen mills at Kabul and Kanda-

Soviet-built installations at Kabul, Afghanistan: above, oil storage tanks; below, bakery, silo, and administration building. (The road in the picture below was paved by the U.S.S.R.)

hār, according to the recommendations of two Polish experts who inspected the plants in the autumn of 1957.

Although Afghan officials were initially very confident of their ability to make good bargains with the bloc countries, there is evidence to suggest that they have become somewhat disillusioned by the high prices charged for Soviet surveys, the costly nature of suggested construction contracts, and the slow pace of visible progress achieved with the funds spent to date. Among those projects which have been completed, some are of disappointing quality, such as the new pavement on the streets of Kabul and the bread produced in the Kabul bakery. On a number of projects previously surveyed by Western business concerns, irritation has been engendered by the Soviet practice of making a complete new survey at much greater cost and recommending schemes far in excess of the relatively cheap original proposals. Because of the high cost of Soviet projects and concern over the future ability of the Afghan Government to finance the local costs of the projects and loan repayments, it seems unlikely that Afghanistan will accept additional credits for some time to come.

Technical Training. More bloc technicians are at work in Afghanistan than in any other country of the free world. Of the 455 bloc technicians working on developmental projects, more than 90 percent are Soviet personnel, the balance being Czechoslovak. In addition the U.S.S.R. has a number of military specialists engaged in training Afghans in the use of Soviet arms. The contrast between the large number of technicians and the paucity of projects under actual construction is due to the high degree of specialization of most Soviet technicians, a condition which requires the use of an unusually large number of men on each survey, and to the retention of Soviet operating personnel on some completed projects such as the Kabul bakery.

Whereas great stress has been placed in Soviet propaganda on the absence of any political strings to Soviet aid, the corollary effort to appear businesslike by charging for all the housing, transportation, gasoline, and amenities used by Soviet technicians has made the presence of so many bloc technicians a heavy burden on Afghanistan. Only a handful of Afghans have gone to bloc countries for technical training.

Trade. The U.S.S.R. is Afghanistan's largest single source for imports and is a close second to India as a market for Afghan exports. Although it is geographically the most accessible market only for northern Afghanistan, the U.S.S.R. has sought to channel as much trade as possible from the whole country to or through the Soviet Union. Its trade is based on annual renewals of a barter agreement of 1950 and on a transit agreement of June 28, 1955. Under the latter agreement, the Soviets have attempted to capture as much of the transit trade to the West, the Far East, and even India as possible and they have been abetted by friction between Afghanistan and Pakistan. A Soviet trade agency has functioned for a number of years in Afghanistan and the U.S.S.R. has had an adviser attached to the Afghan petroleum monopoly.

Afghanistan's dependence on the U.S.S.R. is most marked in oil, the great bulk of which is brought in from the Soviet Union. Other goods purchased in large quantities from the U.S.S.R. are cotton piece goods, priced very low, and sugar, cement, and metal goods. In turn the U.S.S.R. constitutes one of Afghanistan's most important outlets for its principal exports of skins, wool, and raw cotton.

As far as the general public is concerned, the principal impact of bloc trade has probably been the large quantity of Soviet cloth and other consumer goods that has been displayed in Afghan stores, plus some bicycles purchased from Communist China. The only bloc country other than the U.S.S.R. with which Afghanistan has a trade agreement is Czechoslovakia. Trade with the other bloc countries is insignificant.

Ceylon

Significant economic relations between Ceylon and the Sino-Soviet bloc were initiated on December 10, 1952, when Ceylon signed a 5-year agreement with Communist China to sell 50,000 tons of rubber per year and to purchase 270,000 tons of rice at favorable prices. A principal cause of the agreement was the United Nations embargo of May 1951 on shipments of strategic materials to Communist China, which had cut off that country from its supply of rubber. Ceylon, not then a United Nations member, acted because it was facing a marked decline in world prices for its high-cost rubber and a tight, high-priced market in which to buy rice. The first agreement with a bloc country for the provision of economic and technical assistance was concluded on August 16, 1956, with Czechoslovakia. An economic aid agreement and a bilateral trade agreement were concluded with the U.S.S.R. in February 1958.

Credit and Technical Assistance. Under the 3-year agreement with Czechoslovakia, Ceylon is to receive machinery and other goods for industrial projects, and the Czechoslovaks are to supply scientific and technical assistance for the projects selected. Although substantial down payments are called for on the Czechoslovak goods, payment of the balances due may be deferred for a medium term at a 3 percent rate of interest. Although it was understood that the Czechoslovaks would buy an equivalent value of Ceylonese goods, there is no guaranty to that effect, and Ceylon is obligated to pay whatever adverse balance remains in foreign exchange. In sum the terms of this agreement do not appear to be as generous as those usually offered in bloc agreements.

The only project on which agreement has been reached under this agreement is the construction and equipment of a sugar factory at Kantalai, with a capacity of 20,000 tons of white sugar a year and a crushing capacity of 1,200 tons a day. This contract to the value of $3.4 million, signed on January 16, 1958, was the result of the Czechoslovak Tekhnoeksport Corporation offering the lowest bid for construction. Czechoslovak experts have made a survey of the possibilities of constructing one or two cement plants. They have been requested also to advise the government on the possibilities for a hydroelectric station and a fertilizer plant. A proposed ilmenite refinery has been the object of rather tentative Czechoslovak investigation. The delegation which negotiated the agreement in August 1956 also offered to give as a grant bus facilities worth about $64,000 to help Ceylon in its nationalization of buses, but the grant has yet to be made.

On September 19, 1957, at the time a new 5-year trade agreement with Communist China was concluded, a second agreement for economic assistance was also signed providing a Communist Chinese grant of $15.8 million over the 5 years 1958–62 for Ceylon's rubber tree replanting program. On March 3, 1958, Communist China offered and the Ceylonese Prime Minister accepted a further loan of $10.5 million, payable in four equal annual installments and repayable over 10 years at 2.5 percent interest, for rehabilitation of some of the damage caused by heavy floods.

In August 1957 the U.S.S.R. agreed to provide the machinery and technicians to clear 6,000 acres of jungle at Kantalai for the cultivation of sugar cane to supply the projected Czechoslovak crushing plant there. The following month, both the U.S.S.R. and Hungary offered to sell Ceylon a modern, fully automatic telephone exchange valued at about $12 million, but it is not clear whether either offer included credit. On February 25, 1958, the U.S.S.R. concluded an economic aid agreement with Ceylon including a credit of $28.4 million, with terms calling for repayment in 12 years beginning 1 year after delivery in either Ceylonese goods or in convertible currency as agreed upon. Interest will be 2.5 percent. The credit will cover development projects and flood rehabilitation work. The U.S.S.R. will also provide technical assistance and training. Sino-Soviet aid to Ceylon totaled almost $60 million as of March 3, 1958.[1]

Few bloc technicians have as yet started work in Ceylon although Czechoslovak and Soviet technicians will probably commence operations on the Kantalai project in the near future. There are no Ceylonese receiving technical training in bloc countries at the present time.

Trade With the Bloc. In 1956 the two-way trade in rice and rubber with Communist China to the total value of $64 million comprised almost all of Ceylon's trade with the Sino-Soviet bloc. It represented 9.1 percent of Ceylon's total trade, whereas the value of all other trade with the bloc amounted to only 0.6 percent of the total. In October 1957 the U.S.S.R. entered the Ceylon tea market for the first time in 21 years with substantial purchases at auction. On February 8, 1958, a trade and payments agreement was signed with the U.S.S.R. providing for a swing credit of $840,000 and payment of any excess in cash within 1 month. Although quantities were not specified, the principal Ceylonese exports listed are tea, rubber, coconut products, citronella oil, and spices; and its major imports are to be petroleum products, rolled iron and steel products, chemicals, chemical fertilizers, cement, sawn timber, cellulose, cotton textiles, and machinery.

Although by its 5-year trade agreement with Communist China in 1952 Ceylon acted contrary to the United Nations embargo, the rice-rubber deal was initially of economic advantage to both countries. Later, as world rubber prices rose above those stipulated in the original agreement and rice became more available from traditional Southeast Asian sources, the agreement became

[1] Forty million dollars of this amount was accepted after February 1, 1958, and is therefore not included in Table 2, p. 23.

a burden to Ceylon. Commencing in 1955, therefore, Communist China began to pay premiums for rubber according to a sliding scale based on average prices in Singapore. Irrespective of these subsequent developments, the agreement at the outset recognized that a balance would accrue in favor of Ceylon which might be settled in sterling or by the sale of additional commodities to Ceylon. The Ceylonese wanted to purchase additional commodities and sent a trade mission to Communist China for the purpose in March 1957, but it was found that Communist China simply did not have what Ceylon wanted and very little else was imported. As a result, Communist China made cash payments totaling about $38 million during the life of the agreement.

On September 19, 1957, a new 5-year agreement was signed, calling for a lower volume of trade of 200,000 tons of rice per year for 30,000 tons of rubber on a straight sale basis without premium payments or balances to the credit of either side. Although it is thus protected against rising rice prices, which are to be expected during 1958, and against falling rubber prices, Ceylon has no opportunity in this portion of its trade to take advantage of reverse trends. It did receive a $15.8 million grant, however, in lieu of the premium prices for its rubber it had received under the earlier agreement.

In March 1957 Czechoslovakia staged an industrial exhibit in Colombo that was successful in stimulating interest and drawing crowds. The Czechoslovaks are also the only bloc country to have opened a permanent trade office in Ceylon. In January 1958, however, this office was abolished when its functions were transferred to the commercial section of the new Czechoslovak Embassy.

Ceylon has trade agreements with the U.S.S.R., Bulgaria, Czechoslovakia, Hungary, Poland, and Rumania as well as with Communist China. Half of Ceylon's imports from the bloc, excluding Communist China, have come from Czechoslovakia and another third from Poland, but even so the imports from these two countries make up an insignificant fraction (0.5 percent) of Ceylon's total imports.

Ceylon would probably be willing to buy more from the bloc if any attractive offers were made, but until the end of 1957 when the U.S.S.R. started to show an interest in expanding trade, the only significant interest shown by bloc countries in Ceylon's commodities has been the Communist Chinese contract for rubber. The principal complaint engendered by trade with the Sino-Soviet bloc has been that of private Ceylonese traders against the policy of their government of excluding them from all trade with Communist China. In December 1957 the government lifted its control over this trade except for that under the rubber-rice agreement.

India

India's economic relations with the Sino-Soviet bloc were at first confined to trade, in which Communist China played the predominant role in 1951 and 1952. Nevertheless, such trade represented only a small fraction of India's total international commerce and had little effect upon India's traditional economic ties to the West. It was not until the U.S.S.R. offered to build and equip a steel plant at Bhilai that the bloc began to play a significant role in India's economy. That agreement, concluded in February 1955, was the first major offer of economic and technical assistance made by the U.S.S.R. to any non-Communist country. It was welcomed by India because it not only helped to satisfy one of the top priority requirements of India's developmental program but also offered more favorable terms than those secured in 1953 from Krupps-Demag of Germany for the steel plant at Rourkela. The favorable impression created by these terms and by the generally harmonious working relationship established at Bhilai facilitated Indian acceptance of the U.S.S.R.'s second large loan proposal of $126 million tendered in November 1956.

The initiative for these loans appears to have been taken by the U.S.S.R., but India has exercised a controlling voice in the determination of the use to which the second loan is to be put, even though some of the projects were recommended by Soviet teams of experts invited by the Indian Government to survey specific developmental needs. On the other hand, the deferred payment arrangements of other credits with the bloc were probably adopted at the urging of Indian negotiators anxious to conserve foreign exchange during the Second Five-Year Plan. In its trade with the bloc, India has actively sought imports to fill its requirements, while offsetting exports seem to have been stimulated more by the activities of bloc trade missions than by Indian promotional efforts. In part, the bloc has sought to bring its imports from India into better balance with its exports and, in part, it has used large orders for the products of depressed areas as a means of cultivating goodwill.

Credits and Grants. India has accepted almost $300 million in credits from the Sino-Soviet bloc, of which $258.3 million has been in interest-bearing loans from the U.S.S.R. and the balance in deferred payment arrangements. The total amount of grant assistance, other than that contributed through the United Nations Technical Assistance Administration, has been less than $2 million.

The first concrete assistance to India by the U.S.S.R. after several years of vague gestures was the agreement of February 2, 1955, to supervise the construction and to supply the equipment for an integrated iron and steel plant at Bhilai in Madhya Pradesh. Under a supplementary agreement of May 26, 1956, the U.S.S.R. agreed to supply 60,000 tons of structural steel for the plant. The Soviet contribution of $115.5 million in machinery and other equipment and $16.8 million in structural steel is financed by a loan to be repaid in 12 annual installments at an interest rate of 2.5 percent in rupees freely convertible into sterling. The plant will have a capacity of 1 million ingot tons and 750,000 tons of rolled products, and is scheduled to be in operation by 1959. Soviet supplies have arrived on schedule and, although certain phases of construction appear to be lagging, Indian officials in their public statements appear to be satisfied with the rate of progress. In June 1957 the foundation for a 185-foot-high blast furnace was laid. The railroad line to the ore mine was reported to be well under construction, and the diesel power station to supply power for construction was said to be in operation. In September coke and chemical equipment were shipped. In October it was reported that the U.S.S.R. had shipped a 5,000-ton automatic blooming mill installation. A rail and structural steel mill and a continuous billet mill for Bhilai were also reported to be under construction in the U.S.S.R.

In November 1956 the U.S.S.R. offered an additional $126 million credit, but it was not until a year later, on November 9, 1957, that an agreement was reached on the specific projects for which this loan would be used. These are a heavy machinery plant with a capacity of 45,000 tons and a coal mining machinery plant with a capacity of 30,000 tons ($55.7 million); a 250,000 kilowatt thermal electric power station at Neiveli ($33.6 million); a factory for the manufacture of optical glass (50 tons) and ophthalmic glass (250 tons) ($1.8 million); development of the Korba coalfields ($16.8 million); with a balance of $18.2 million as a cushion against price increases. The projects for the Korba coalfields were designated in four supplementary agreements with the National Coal Development Corporation, signed on December 14, 1957, as an open cast mine, two or three other coal mines in the vicinity of Korba, a central workshop for the repair and maintenance of coal mining equipment, and a coal washing and dressing plant. The credit is similar to that for Bhilai in carrying 2.5 percent interest and in being repayable in 12 annual installments, but payment will not begin until a year after the delivery of the entire equipment for each project. Therefore, India is not expected to have to begin repayments until after the conclusion of its current Second Five-Year Plan (March 31, 1961).

At the time that the Bhilai steel plant agreement was being negotiated, in January 1955, the Soviets also offered to extend a credit for modernizing the Panna diamond mines in Vindhya Pradesh which had been surveyed by two Soviet mining experts, but this offer was not accepted.

In September 1957 Prime Minister Nehru announced that India had received a Soviet offer for an additional loan of $25 million for the construction of pharmaceutical factories. To date, no action has been taken on this offer.

In January 1958 India requested an additional credit of $31.5 million for the Bhilai plant to cover price increases and the import of materials, which it had originally expected to produce locally. The U.S.S.R. has not acceded to this request.

To date, therefore, the credits for Bhilai and the $126 million credit obligated in November 1957, a total of $258.3 million, constitute the interest-bearing obligations of India to the Soviet Union. It would appear, however, that a deferred payment arrangement may have been involved in two agreements concluded in May 1956 and a supplementary agreement signed on May 11, 1957, under which India agreed to purchase from the U.S.S.R. equipment to a value of about $3.6 million for its oil exploration program. This consists of three oil-drilling rigs, tools, accessories, and related cement and workshop facilities. The first Soviet drilling rig had penetrated to a depth of 5,200 feet at Jawalamukhi in East Punjab at the end of 1957.

The only grant assistance from the Soviet Union, other than token relief shipments of food, has been the gift in 1956 of 69 tractors, other agricultural machinery, an automatic telephone exchange, an electric power station, five mobile workshops, and a number of transport vehicles, the total valued at $1.5 million, for a 5,000-acre central mechanized farm at Suratgarh in Rajasthan.

Czechoslovak acceptance of deferred payments, amounting to a medium term loan, was involved in at least part of the cost of $1.9 million in an agreement

Iron and steel plant under construction at Bhilai, India, under Soviet supervision.

made by Skoda of Czechoslovakia with the Assam Cooperative Sugar Mills, Ltd. to erect and equip Assam's first sugar refinery, with a daily capacity of about 1,000 tons. This agreement was approved by the Government of India on July 26, 1956. On January 4, 1958, during Premier Siroky's visit to India, an agreement was signed whereby the Czechoslovak Government would loan India the foreign exchange component of about $34 million for India's $63 million foundry-forge project at Ranchi, Bihar, which is to have an annual capacity of 45,000 tons. The loan is to be repaid in eight semiannual installments commencing in 1961.

In addition, deferred payments appear to have been involved at least in part in the following Czechoslovak projects: (1) the erection and equipment of a sugar refinery at Panipat, Punjab, according to an agreement concluded at the end of 1955 between the Punjab State Government and Skoda; (2) the construction and equipment of a cement factory with an initial daily capacity of 200 tons at Cherrapunji, Assam, according to an agreement reached in early 1956 between Assam Cement, Ltd. of Calcutta and the Czechoslovak Technoexport foreign trade corporation ($2.1 million); and (3) equipment for an electric power station at Surat, Bombay, on which agreement was reached in early 1956.

Also included within this category is an agreement of December 18, 1956, between the Cekop firm of Poland and Indian Champaka Sugar Plantations, Ltd. for the establishment of a sugar refinery at Mannargudi, Tanjore, with a crushing capacity of 800 tons daily. In July 1957 India obtained a deferred payment arrangement on the purchase of $2.5 million worth of textile machinery from East Germany. On March 19, 1956, an agreement was concluded between the Governments of India and Rumania for the purchase of a petroleum drilling rig ($840,000), the operational supervision by 21 Rumanian technicians, and the training of Indian technicians to operate it ($115,000). The drill went into operation in April 1957 but was replaced in September by the faster "turbo drill" received from the U.S.S.R.

East Germany has shown an interest in lignite mining and the newsprint industry and has offered to establish a raw-film industry in India at a cost of about $10.5 million.

Thus of the almost $300 million in credits extended to India by the Sino-Soviet bloc, the Soviet Union and Czechoslovakia contributed over 98 percent. The absence of Communist China is notable. Also noteworthy is the fact that most of these credits were for industrial projects, with primacy given to heavy industry. This approach has pleased Indian officials because of the high priority placed on heavy industry in the current Second Five-Year Plan. Besides giving assistance to projects accorded top priority by the Indian Government, the bloc has tended to concentrate its aid on a limited number of fairly large projects with visible appeal. For both reasons, it has succeeded in stimulating more attention than the total amount of aid might appear to warrant.

In general, bloc projects appear to make a sizable contribution to India's industrial development program. Indian officials have expressed satisfaction with the rate of progress maintained on these projects, and there seems to be little cause for complaint on the bloc's performance to date, except for the disappointing pace set by the Rumanian oil rig. Not all projects recommended by bloc experts have been accepted by the Indian Government, however, and some phases of construction of the Bhilai steel mill may be somewhat behind schedule.

Technical Training. It is estimated that there were about 260 bloc technicians in India for 1 month or more during the last 6 months of 1957. Of these almost two-thirds were from the Soviet Union. Of the remainder, all from the European satellites, the greatest number were from Czechoslovakia. A large proportion of the developmental projects for which India has received credits from the Soviet bloc involves technical training or has been predicated on the findings of bloc scientists and engineers. For example, it was on the basis of reports by teams of five Soviet experts each that the agreement on petroleum exploration was concluded and that the Korba coalfield project and the coal mining machinery plant were decided upon. In January 1957, 26 topographers, geophysicists, and engineers arrived from the Soviet Union, and it was on the basis of the immediate success of some of these experts that drilling operations started at Jawalamukhi. Eight officers of the Indian Oil Commission are receiving training from the Rumanian experts there. Among the projects under way, the Bhilai steel plant involves the greatest number of bloc technicians and engineers. The number will rise as actual work commences on the projects included under the second Soviet loan.

Bloc technicians appear to have been carefully selected to make a good impression and have succeeded in doing so by their technical competence, cooperative behavior, and frank, affable manner. Perhaps their greatest asset has been the absence of condescension, through stressing cooperation rather than aid, and avoiding boasts about the superiority of Communist countries.

Bloc experts have also been involved in surveying other projects which have either not been approved so far or have been executed without further bloc assistance. In this category may be placed a survey of India's copper-bearing areas by two Soviet experts, the recommendations of two Soviet mining engineers on the development of the Panna diamond mines, and an aerial survey made by Czechoslovaks of a remote section of Assam in conjunction with plans to build a 78-mile ropeway. Poland has also evinced an interest in helping India develop its copper resources, and both Poland and Hungary have offered to help in lignite mining. At the invitation of the Indian Government, a number of experts such as the well-known Polish economist, Oscar Lange, have visited India, but their services have been for limited periods only. A delegation of Soviet farmers in November 1957 recommended large-scale mechanization of Indian farming. Chinese Communist missions, which have included an agricultural delegation and a forestry and a salt mission, have come to learn rather than to extend assistance.

The most important bloc program for training Indians abroad is that under the Bhilai steel agreement, under which about 700 skilled workers, engineers, and technicians are to receive supplementary training in the U.S.S.R. after preliminary training in India. Of this number, about 180 have been sent to

Soviet workers of the State Institute for Iron and Steel Works Planning review plans for the iron and steel plant at Bhilai, India.

the U.S.S.R., some of whom have already returned, and others will probably go to the Soviet Union in the near future. Under the auspices of the United Nations Technical Assistance Administration, eight officers of the Indian Oil Commission left on December 4, 1956, to receive practical training at Soviet oilfields. According to press reports a few others may have gone for specialized training in geophysics and geology. Technical training does not appear to have been provided to Indians in other bloc countries.

As in the case of bloc technicians sent to India, there does not appear to have been any conscious attempt to mix political propaganda with the technical training received by Indians sent to the Soviet Union. In conformity with its neutralist policy, the Indian Government has excluded political considerations from its judgment of training offers.

Trade With the Bloc. In the 5 years 1952 through 1956, Indian imports from the Sino-Soviet bloc have grown from $38.8 million to $72.3 million, and exports to the bloc have risen from $12.7 million to $49.4 million. This increase represents a rise from 2.3 percent of total Indian imports to 4.3 percent, and from 1 percent of total exports to 3.9 percent. The direction of trade has shown a marked shift within the bloc, from a position in which five-sixths of India's imports from the bloc came from Communist China in 1952 and half of India's exports to the bloc went to China to a pattern in 1956 in which China accounted for less than 30 percent of India's imports from the bloc, in comparison to 42.5 percent for the U.S.S.R., and for only a quarter of India's exports to the bloc, as compared to more than half for the U.S.S.R. Although figures for most of 1957 are not yet available, they will probably show a substantial rise over those for the previous year. The State Trading Corporation has handled about 20 percent of this trade.

India's trade with the U.S.S.R. has been governed by (1) a 5-year trade agreement signed on December 2, 1953; (2) a separate agreement, announced December 13, 1955, providing for the import over the 3-year period 1956–58 of 1 million tons of Soviet iron and steel plus oil drilling, mining, and other equipment in exchange for Indian commodities of a total value equal to the iron and steel; and (3) noncommercial imports financed by the U.S.S.R. for the developmental projects for which the Soviet Union has extended credits. To date, India's principal imports from the U.S.S.R. have been iron and steel, machinery, wheat, barley, and printing paper, and its chief exports to the U.S.S.R. have been hides and skins, wool, jute manufactures, lac, tea, coffee, pepper, and cashew nuts. However, marked changes in the composition of Soviet purchases have occurred. In 1956, for example, the U.S.S.R. bought Indian tea for the first time in several years and did so to the tune of millions of dollars. It also bought 500 tons of coffee and has reportedly contracted to buy 725 more tons. In 1957 exports of $2.5 million worth of handmade Indian shoes commenced, plus 250,000 yards of woolen gabardine and a large order for woolen hosiery. Of late, Soviet trade officials have shown an increasing interest in purchasing Kashmiri handicrafts.

In some instances, this variation in purchases has served to bolster weak markets, as in the case of an order for cashew nuts in July 1956 and large purchases of pepper in the winter of 1956–57. Thereby the Soviets have not only taken advantage of low prices but have also had some success in making a favorable impression on such producing areas as the state of Kerala, which has a Communist government.

Certain Indian purchases other than the million tons of steel are worthy of note. An order for 15 broad-gauge steam locomotive boilers, valued at $182,000, was placed in mid-1956. In August 1957 the State Trading Corporation decided to buy 500 Soviet tractors, and the Indian press speculates that in the near future India will be purchasing substantial quantities of earth-moving equipment and road-rollers. It is also rumored that India may obtain about 12,000 cotton textile spindles on a deferred payment basis. The purchase of Soviet coal mining equipment has already been negotiated on a deferred payments basis.

Under India's trade agreement with Communist China, signed October 14, 1954, trade has grown from a mere $10.8 million in 1953 to more than $33 million in 1956, but this latter figure remains well below those for 1951 and 1952 (1952 saw a total of over $44 million). The export surplus enjoyed during the first 2 years has turned to a deficit because of increasing Indian imports of iron and steel manufactures and a decline in India's exports of raw cotton and jute goods. India's principal imports by sea and air are iron and steel (over 45 percent of the total in 1956), newsprint, caustic soda and soda ash, raw silk, and spices. Under a separate agreement signed on August 28, 1956, India bought 60,000 tons of rice. India's principal exports by these routes are raw cotton, jute manufactures, tobacco, pepper, and lac. From Tibet, India imports overland a considerable amount of wool and other animal hair (about $2.7 million in 1956) and to Tibet it sends primarily cotton goods, woolen cloth, stationery, iron and steel, and foodstuffs. Altogether, Tibet accounted for $9.7 million of the trade with Communist China in 1956.

The overseas trade is channelled through the China National Native Produce Corporation of Peiping, with the Shanghai branch of that corporation handling the actual export transactions. On the Indian side, all of the caustic soda, soda ash, and raw silk have been imported by the State Trading Corporation. The Indian market has shown satisfaction with the quality and promptness of Chinese deliveries, but the most important reason for the expansion of imports would seem to be prices that are lower than those of Western suppliers. Tibet has paid for so-called essential commodities such as petroleum, cement, and iron and steel products with Chinese silver dollars.

India's principal imports from Czechoslovakia have been machinery, particularly for sugar refining, printing paper, and chemicals. In the last trade year (1956–57), 40,000 tons of steel were to have been imported, and in November 1957 the Indian railroad purchasing mission bought 20,000 tons of steel. Almost three quarters of Czechoslovak imports from India have consisted of iron ore, the other major items being goat skins and pepper. The current 3-year agreement, signed on September 30, 1957, provides for triangular trade and payments, by which Czechoslovakia may transfer its rupee balances to countries like Egypt and Indonesia with which it has adverse balances and which would like to use the rupees for imports from India.

From Poland, India has imported principally machinery and metals. By the end of 1956, 2,600 freight cars had been imported. In that year, 30 broad-gauge steam locomotives valued at $2.5 million were ordered. The trade agreement signed in April 1956 called for imports of 300,000 tons of Polish iron and steel products over a 3-year period and purchases by Poland of an equal quantity of iron ore. Imports from Hungary are also principally machinery and metals. Three quarters of Hungary's purchases from India in 1956 consisted of raw wool. From East Germany, India imports chemicals, chiefly ammonium sulphate. In mid-1956 India placed an order for 17 special freight cars capable of transporting heavy plant and machinery valued at $200,000. In July 1957 India obtained a deferred payment agreement on the purchase of $2.5 million worth of East German textile machinery. Cement promises to supplant machinery and metals in imports from Rumania. The principal import from North Viet-Nam has been rice.

Most bloc countries maintain commercial representatives in India's key cities. Their most distinctive promotional efforts, however, take the form of displays of their wares, especially at trade fairs. For example, the official Chinese trade representation maintains showrooms in New Delhi, Bombay, and Calcutta. It does not employ traveling salesmen nor indulge in newspaper advertising but shows particular interest in trade fairs, where many consumer articles have been shown despite the small volume of consumer imports from China.

Although India has bilateral trade agreements with every country in the Sino-Soviet bloc except Albania, 90 percent of its total imports of $72.3 million from the bloc in 1956 and 92 percent of its total exports of $49.4 million were accounted for by the U.S.S.R., Communist China, and Czechoslovakia.

The first such trade agreements were concluded with Czechoslovakia, Poland, and Hungary in 1948 and 1949. The last agreement, signed in August 1957, was a semiofficial one with the trading organizations of North Korea, a country whose government is not recognized by India. In making these agreements, the Indian Government has pursued four principles of trade policy: (1) nondiscrimination, (2) the issuance of import licenses purely on currency considerations on the basis of multilateral trade within a currency area, (3) nonacceptance of quotas for specific destinations, and (4) avoidance, as far as possible, of bilateral balancing or barter. Accordingly, India has generally refused to accept specific quotas for imports and exports. Balances due either party are payable in pounds sterling. In its present foreign exchange difficulties, India has been attempting to obtain agreement to settlement in rupees and has been successful in this effort with Communist China, Czechoslovakia, East Germany, and Hungary. In a further effort to save exchange, India has recently tried to arrange for deferred payments on its imports. Although it has not as yet met with significant success, it is aided in its efforts by an increasing amount of competition among the members of the Sino-Soviet bloc.

In order to deal more effectively with the state trading organizations of the bloc and to bring its exports to the bloc into better balance with its imports, the Indian Government organized the State Trading Corporation in May 1956. Although this corporation has had a monopoly on trade in certain commodities, it still controls only a minor part of the trade with the bloc, and imports continue to be far in excess of exports.

To facilitate trade, India has also concluded shipping agreements with the U.S.S.R. and Poland. The Indo-Soviet agreement of April 6, 1956, established direct service between the Indian ports of Bombay and Calcutta and the Soviet ports of Odessa and Novorossisk by six Soviet and six Indian vessels with a total of about 55,000 gross registered tons. Under this agreement, it was expected that 350,000 tons of Soviet commodities would be received by India annually. Under the Polish agreement of May 16, 1956, three ships of each country were selected to carry the seaborne commerce between the two countries.

A direct air link to Prague was opened in April 1956 by Air India International. Repeated negotiations with the U.S.S.R. have finally led to agreement on a direct air route to Moscow, but nothing has come of Communist Chinese efforts to promote an air route to Peiping.

Having found bloc products to be generally satisfactory, Indians are not reluctant to expand their trade with the bloc, although they would be averse to becoming dependent upon the bloc. So far there are only a few commodities in which disruption of trade with the bloc would seriously affect Indian markets. Among Indian exports of significant value in 1956, the bloc took 37.8 percent of hides and skins, 24.4 percent pepper, and 24.3 percent of iron ore, while India imported from the bloc 23.4 percent of its total imports of printing paper, 22.5 percent of the grain imported, and 10.3 percent of the iron and steel.

Nepal

The Kingdom of Nepal is torn between its desire for external assistance, its fear that political strings may be attached to offers of aid from the Sino-Soviet bloc, its desire to continue trade with Tibet to the north, and the need to maintain good commercial and political relations with India to the south, which is sensitive to any bloc penetration in Nepal that might threaten its own security.

Although the U.S.S.R. has made some vague offers of assistance, the only country in the bloc with which Nepal has concluded any economic agreements is Communist China. A trade and friendship agreement was signed in September 1956 following the arrival of a six-member Communist Chinese trade delegation, and a few weeks later, on October 7, 1956, on the conclusion of the then Nepalese Prime Minister's visit to Peiping, the Communist Chinese government announced that it would grant Nepal $12.6 million over a 3-year period. Both accords were agreeable to the Nepalese Government of that time, but Nepalese interest in the trade agreement appears to have flagged in view of their procrastination in giving it effect.

Bloc Assistance. On February 3, 1957, Nepal received on schedule the first installment of $2 million of Peiping's cash grant of $12.6 million. A second installment of approximately the same amount was received in February 1958, and the balance of the grant is to be received in the form of machinery, raw materials, and other commodities during 1959 and 1960. There is no indication that any of the first installment has yet been used for development projects. However, there do not appear to have been any specific conditions attached to the use of the cash allotments.

Peiping's aid offer did not provide for Chinese technicians to be sent to Nepal. No bloc technicians are working in Nepal, nor are Nepalese receiving technical training in bloc countries.

Trade With the Bloc. Although probably second in importance to its trade with India, Nepal's trade with Tibet is not very large, amounting in all likelihood to no more than a tenth of its total trade. Its principal imports have been salt and wool, and its principal exports to Tibet ground wheat, rice, and ground peas. If and when a hard-surface road is completed between Katmandu and the Tibetan border, the volume of trade will probably increase. Fulfillment of the terms of the trade agreement with Communist China could also probably stimulate additional trade, since the accord called for the reciprocal establishment of trade agencies on both sides of the border and specifically for a Communist Chinese consulate general at Katmandu as well as three Communist Chinese agencies with diplomatic privileges in outlying districts of Nepal. The agreement was not ratified until January 17, 1958, and India has consistently sought to persuade the Nepalese Government to continue to postpone the establishment of the Communist Chinese consulate general and agencies. Having ratified the treaty, however, Katmandu may find it more difficult to resist pressure from Peiping to give effect to the agreement.

IX. LATIN AMERICA

Argentina

Following conclusion of a trade agreement with Argentina in 1953, the U.S.S.R. entered this market for the first time on a substantial scale while the satellites also increased their purchases and sales in the Argentine market. In 1954–55 Argentine trade with the bloc averaged $175 million per year, or about 9 percent of total Argentine trade, as compared with an average of $35 million in 1952–53. By the end of 1955 increased bloc marketings were keeping pace with larger bloc purchases and had reduced accumulated trade debits. In mid-1955 the U.S.S.R. held a trade exhibit featuring a wide variety of industrial equipment in Buenos Aires, its first exhibit in Latin America.

With the overthrow of Peron in September 1955, bloc trade, which had been largely on a government-to-government basis, faded as rapidly as it had grown. Argentina's new provisional government sought to strengthen economic ties with the free world through settlement of outstanding debts and through multilateral trade arrangements and to liquidate state trade operations. Trade totals with the bloc dropped to about $100 million in 1956 and to less than $50 million in 1957. However, as serious payments problems continued, and since the bloc had trade debts to Argentina, the Argentine provisional government dispatched a mission to the bloc in January 1958.

Credits. The bloc countries have not so far made concrete large-scale offers of credits to Argentina, although such offers are periodically rumored, especially with regard to petroleum supply and development. In the Soviet trade and payments agreements of 1953, Argentina was offered a Soviet credit of $30 million. This was not used, and was scaled down to $4 million in a 1955 protocol, under which Argentina apparently purchased $660,000 in machinery during 1956. Of a similar Czechoslovak credit of $15 million in a 1955 agreement, Argentina used $2 million. Argentine agreements of 1957 with Czechoslovakia, Hungary, and Poland provide for bloc financing of Argentine purchases of capital goods, but without specifying the amount of credit that might be made available. No other offers are known to be pending at this time. Over the long run Argentina has been the trade creditor of the bloc countries and has not gained any significant developmental credits from the bloc.

The Czechoslovak credit of $2 million extended to Argentina covered capital equipment for a coal-washing plant at the government-owned Rio Turbio mines. While terms under this credit extended to 6 years, repayment of 75 percent is due by completion date, now scheduled for late 1958, with the remainder to be paid by 1961. In effect this is a commercial line of credit, although with more liberal terms than usually available, rather than a development credit such as the bloc countries have granted to other areas.

Technical Training. No large number of bloc technicians accompanied the increased commercial interchange between the bloc and Argentina, and all but a few of those who entered Argentina came in connection with contracts made by government agencies, the only important purchasers of bloc machinery and equipment. It is estimated that about 40 bloc technicians were in the country at the end of 1957.

Six Czechoslovak technicians were scheduled to arrive in Argentina to supervise installation of the Rio Turbio coal-washing plant.

Hungarian technicians have accompanied shipments of Ganz railroad equipment purchased by the Argentine state railways in the postwar years. As many as 40 such technicians have worked in Argentina during this period. The Hungarian bid to supply 300 Ganz self-propelled diesel cars to the state railways included an offer of another 250 technicians. Ultimately decision was made to contract for only 90 Ganz cars.

There is no known program of providing technical training to Argentina in the bloc.

Trade. In 1957 bloc trade with Argentina stood at less than $50 million, a sharp decline from the $161 million of 1954 and the peak of $189 million in 1955. Since 1953 the U.S.S.R. has joined Czechoslovakia, Hungary, and Poland as a major partner in Argentina's trade with the bloc, and Soviet trade contributed heavily to the 1954–55 peak through shipments of petroleum and iron and steel products and purchases of hides and meat. Bloc-Argentine trade has consisted largely of bulk commodities. Argentina ships hides, meat, grain, wool, linseed oil, quebracho extract, and other raw materials. Bloc sales to Argentina have included petroleum products, coal, iron sheet, steel bars, rails, aluminum ingots, cement, lumber, wood pulp, and other industrial materials. In addition the bloc has sold some machinery and equipment to state corporations. The largest single item in Argentine sales to the bloc in recent years has been hides, with about $20 million shipped annually in the period 1954–56. Contributing heavily to the bulge in bloc shipments to Argentina in 1954–56 were exports of coal, petroleum products, rolling stock, and rails—all commodities which normally consume a large part of Argentina's dollar resources.

Trade Promotion. Soviet-bloc efforts to promote trade with Argentina have included the negotiation of bilateral trade and payments agreements which fix trade goals and list items to be exchanged, bloc trade exhibits, and trade missions to Argentina.

Bloc trade promotion efforts have failed to stimulate private business interest in bloc merchandise, even when free-world goods cannot be imported and bloc currencies are readily available. Consequently, Argentine state corporations provide the market for the greater part of bloc goods shipped to this country including petroleum to YPF, coal to state power plants, rails to the municipal transport system, and rolling stock to state railroads. Under

Peron, the state trading corporation (IAPI) bought and distributed Skoda trucks and other equipment to the private sector, forcing the goods on the market, but this outlet for bloc merchandise was eliminated with the overthrow of Peron.

Trade and Payments Agreements. Argentina has trade and payments agreements with five bloc countries—the U.S.S.R., Czechoslovakia, Hungary, Poland, and Rumania.

The Soviet-Argentine trade and payments agreement signed August 1953, as amended in May 1955, provides a total trade goal of $100 million, with a swing credit of $11 million. Under the trade and payments agreements with Czechoslovakia, Hungary, and Poland of October 1957 replacing previous agreements, a total trade goal of $130 million is set, with swing credits amounting to $9.5 million. A new trade and payments agreement with Rumania concluded in January 1958 establishes a swing credit of $2 million; no trade goal has been reported.

In 1954 and 1955 bloc-Argentine trade came near meeting established trade goals of some $200 million. The trade goals were again set at roughly the same level in 1957 revisions even though actual trade was proceeding at less than one-quarter of the goals envisaged. Argentine credit balances under its agreements with the bloc totaled about $18 million in late 1957. An Argentine official trade mission to the bloc sought to use those balances and also to purchase goods up to the amount of the swing credits made available under the various agreements with the bloc.

Brazil

Bloc efforts to expand ties with Brazil were intensified in the closing months of 1957 and have achieved more public prominence than concrete results to date. Soviet officials have sought the resumption of diplomatic relations broken by Brazil in 1947. Brazilian ties with the bloc are now maintained through diplomatic and commercial ties with Czechoslovakia and Poland and trade with Hungary. They have consisted primarily of a limited commercial exchange. However, in line with new Soviet moves, including a November 1957 interview by Khrushchev, which related Brazil's alleged vast trade prospects in the bloc to resumption of diplomatic relations with the U.S.S.R., the satellite missions have been suggesting that new markets can be found for Brazilian exports, principally coffee, which are meeting greater competition in the Western world, with consequent accumulation of unsalable stocks.

Credits. Brazil has apparently not so far received any firm offers of long-term developmental credit or technical assistance from bloc countries, although there have been persistent rumors of such offers. While a Polish credit of $2 million on 4-year terms to a private Brazilian shipping firm for purchase of two cargo vessels may qualify as a developmental credit, other credits have been on a strictly limited commercial basis. To the extent that Brazil has been Poland's creditor under bilateral clearing arrangements, as was the case in 1957, actually no credit to Brazil at all is involved. In their campaign for resumption of Soviet-Brazilian relations, Soviet spokesmen have talked of unlimited markets for Brazilian products. This propaganda in turn has given rise to evidently unfounded rumors of large-scale developmental credits that might be provided by the bloc, were Brazil to resume relations with the U.S.S.R.

Technical Training. There is no known program of providing technical training to Brazilians in the bloc, and there are no formal arrangements for bloc technicians to operate in Brazil.

Trade. Brazilian trade with the bloc doubled between 1954 and 1956, from $43 million, or about 1.3 percent of total trade, to $86 million, or 3.3 percent of the total. In 1957 bloc-Brazilian trade was perhaps 10 percent under the peak attained in 1956. Czechoslovakia, Poland, and Hungary accounted for virtually all of this trade. Bloc purchases from Brazil have included coffee, cacao, raw cotton, hides, and iron ore and have represented a substantial part of total Brazilian exports only in the case of hides, which is not a major export commodity. Bloc sales to Brazil consist of a wide variety of manufactures and raw materials, including chemicals, iron and steel products (bars, ingots, wire, tubes, pipes, rails), cement, and various types of machinery (stationary motors, agricultural equipment, lathes). The biggest single Brazilian import from the bloc has been hops and malt, with steel rails taking the second ranking position in 1957.

Trade Promotion. Soviet-bloc efforts to promote trade with Brazil have been largely limited to the activities of the Czechoslovak and Polish Legations, plus the Hungarian resident commercial mission in Rio de Janeiro. These have been supplemented by occasional traveling bloc trade missions. Rumanian and East German trade offers are reported also to have been made in foreign capitals. With respect to the U.S.S.R., private Brazilian firms purporting to be speaking for their government have, from time to time, announced substantial trade offers without, however, any results to date. Both Czechoslovakia and Poland exhibited at the 1955 São Paulo International Trade Fair and plan participation in the forthcoming Industrial Exposition at Rio.

Trade and Payments Agreements. Brazil has trade and payments agreements with three bloc countries—Czechoslovakia, Poland, and Hungary, dating respectively from 1950, 1952, and 1954. These agreements are now operating under temporary short-term extensions pending the negotiation of new agreements. No negotiations have yet been started on the new agreements. Brazilian objectives are to obtain a greater degree of currency convertibility in their trade with the bloc. There has been some small trade with Communist China and East Germany without any formal agreements and payable in sterling.

Brazil's payments-accords with the bloc follow the standard pattern in establishing payments regulations and setting up clearing accounts in agreement dollars. Swing margins in the agreements total $7 million, including $3 million with Czechoslovakia and $2 million each with Hungary and Poland. Brazil has never, so far as is known, invoked the annual right to claim liquidation of excesses over the swing margins in convertible or other acceptable currencies. Both parties to the agreements set forth trade quotas by commodity but these are more illustrative than mandatory.

In recent years Brazil has had difficulty in maintaining equilibrium in its clearing accounts with the Soviet-bloc countries. The tendency has been for Brazil to build up clearing credits which could not be used, prompting periodic imposition of controls aimed at limiting exports to bloc countries. At the end of 1955 Brazil, in relation to the total trade involved, was a substantial creditor with the three bloc countries with which it has direct trade relations. By the end of 1956 overall bloc accounts were approximately in balance, but by November 1957 the Brazilians were again in a creditor position. In part this situation may be explained by the fact that the trade consists largely of Brazilian exports of raw material and foodstuffs surpluses that can be shipped out of existing stocks and imports by Brazil of long-lead industrial type items from the bloc. Moreover, bloc products, when imported by private traders, often cannot compete with United States or Western European products unless at a highly subsidized rate of exchange. Since, under the exchange auction system in Brazil, the minimum bid for bloc currencies by importers must be at least equal to 80 percent of those for convertible currencies, large amounts of bloc currencies remain unsold and in effect are carried over from auction to auction. When Brazilian balances of bloc currencies go too high, the Bank of Brazil refuses to authorize exports of certain products, especially those which can earn hard currencies, or alternatively may limit exports to compensating imports.

Uruguay

Soviet-bloc efforts to develop trade with Uruguay first yielded significant results in 1954 when the Soviet Union signed a payments agreement with Uruguay and made heavy purchases of meat. Uruguay agreed to increased bloc purchases which, totaling almost 10 percent of the country's exports, provided temporary relief from burdensome export surpluses. While Uruguayan trade with the bloc has been very uneven, the appeal of an alternative market and source of supply has helped the bloc countries to confirm and extend a network of trade and payments agreements with this country.

Credits. There have been unsubstantiated rumors of impending large-scale credits in recent months. Under Uruguayan trade and payments agreements with the bloc there are provisions for swing credits and overdrafts amounting to about $5 million. However, Uruguay has been on balance the trade creditor of the bloc countries.

Technical Training. There is no known program of providing technical training to Uruguayans in the bloc.

Trade. In 1957 the bloc's direct trade with Uruguay totaled about $12.5 million, as compared with $26.4 million in 1954, $13 million in 1955, and $18.6 million in 1956. In addition to direct trade sizable shipments of Uruguayan wool and wool tops reportedly have reached the bloc through third countries.

Including indirect shipments, trade in 1955–56 probably totaled more than $50 million, or about one-eighth of total trade. The drop in trade during 1957, hitting indirect as well as direct shipments, in part reflected an overall slowdown in Uruguayan trade.

In recent years, Czechoslovakia and Poland have been Uruguay's principal bloc partners in direct trade, although in 1954–55 the Soviet Union rose to prominence as the largest bloc trader in Uruguay. Chief Uruguayan exports to the bloc are wool, meat, and hides, which account for 80 percent of Uruguay's total exports. Bloc supplies to Uruguay have consisted primarily of industrial materials, such as cement, chemicals, newsprint, iron and steel piping, and certain raw materials, notably cotton.

The bloc, although it has proved a somewhat erratic market for direct Uruguayan exports, has apparently purchased substantial quantities of Uruguayan wool through third countries. Overall the bloc purchases have helped to remove burdensome surpluses from time to time.

Trade Promotion. Soviet-bloc efforts to promote trade with Uruguay have included negotiations for trade and payments agreements, with conclusion of pacts by all European-bloc countries except Rumania and Albania, and extensive, if inconclusive, negotiations by Communist China. In early 1958 negotiations for a payments pact with Rumania were under way. Although only the Soviet Union, Czechoslovakia, and Rumania maintain diplomatic relations with Uruguay, other bloc countries either maintain permanent trade delegations in Montevideo or operate through traveling missions. The resident missions apparently act directly as sales agents, and advertise in trade journals as such. During 1956 Czechoslovakia staged a well-publicized and well-received industrial exposition in Montevideo, displaying a wide variety of machinery, including tractors, and various consumers goods. Uruguayan participation in trade fairs held by bloc countries has also been encouraged.

Trade and Payments Agreements. Uruguay's trade with the Soviet-bloc area in the postwar period has been governed principally by payments agreements concluded between the Uruguayan Bank of the Republic and banks of bloc countries. In early 1958 the agreements extended to all except Albania, Communist China, and Rumania and were the subject of negotiation with Rumania. The Uruguayan Government has also negotiated government-to-government trade and payments agreements with Czechoslovakia (1955) and the Soviet Union (1956); ratification of the former was completed in 1957. These pacts, which include a commercial treaty, a commercial convention, and a payments agreement, replace the interbank payments agreements and serve to formalize Uruguayan relations with the bloc. While made for a limited period, they are tacitly renewable. One feature of the Czechoslovak and Soviet payments agreements that is presumably attractive to Uruguay is provision for use of account balances in payments to third countries.

X. EUROPE

Iceland

The Soviet-bloc economic offensive in Iceland has been closely geared to the internal political situation and particularly to the defense policies of the country. In the early postwar years, when the Communists were in the Icelandic Government, trade with the U.S.S.R. increased rapidly. In 1947, however, a government was formed which excluded the Communists, and for the next 5 years the U.S.S.R. showed little interest in trade with Iceland.

In 1951 the United States-manned NATO Defense Force activated defense installations in Iceland, and in 1952, in retaliation for Icelandic extension of its territorial waters, United Kingdom fishing interests instituted a landing ban on Icelandic fish in United Kingdom ports. This latter development hastened the transformation of Icelandic fish production from fresh fish to frozen fillets, resulting in an increased need for markets for frozen fish. Seeing here an opportunity to weaken Iceland's NATO orientation, the Soviet Union almost overnight became a major taker of Icelandic frozen fish fillets. In 1952 the bloc accounted for about 7 percent of Iceland's foreign trade, and by 1957 this figure had increased to about 34 percent. During the past year the bloc has intensified its efforts to increase economic penetration through trade and credits.

Credits. In 1956, before the formation of the present government, which includes Communists, Iceland accepted a 7-year commercial credit from Czechoslovakia totaling $1.7 million for the purchase of small hydroelectric units and transformer stations. The credit is to be repaid through Icelandic fish exports to Czechoslovakia, and provision for repayment was incorporated into the 1957 Icelandic-Czechoslovak trade agreement.

Late in 1956 Iceland and East Germany signed an agreement for the construction of five 75-ton fishing boats in East Germany, payable via the Icelandic–East German trade agreement. In 1957 Iceland and East Germany signed a further agreement for the construction in East Germany of twelve 250-ton fishing vessels, at a cost of $3.2 million, repayable over a 4-year period through credits on the Icelandic clearing agreement with East Germany.

In 1957 the U.S.S.R. was reported to have offered Iceland a long-term, low-interest credit totaling $24.5 million. The reported U.S.S.R. credit has not been accepted by Iceland.

Trade. Icelandic trade with the Soviet bloc has shown a considerable increase since 1954. In 1954 Iceland's exports to the bloc were valued at $12.9 million, which was 25 percent of total export value. Imports were valued at $12.7 million, which was 18 percent of the value of total imports. In 1957

Icelandic exports to the bloc of $20.3 million were 34 percent of the value of total exports, while imports valued at $27.8 million were 33 percent of total imports.

The principal bloc trading partners are the U.S.S.R., which accounts for about two-thirds of the total trade volume, Czechoslovakia, and East Germany. The principal Icelandic exports are frozen fish fillets and salted herring. The principal Icelandic imports from the U.S.S.R. are petroleum products, cement, coal and coke, timber, and iron and steel products. From Czechoslovakia the main Icelandic imports are textiles, machinery, hardware, footwear, ceramic and glass products, and vehicles. From East Germany the main imports are sugar, cement, chemicals, diesel engines, machinery, machine tools, and fishing vessels.

Bloc trade promotion efforts have been rather ambitious, considering the small size of the area. In 1955 a Soviet-Czechoslovak-Chinese trade fair was held in Reykjavik, and a Czechoslovak-East German-Rumanian fair was held there in 1957. East Germany opened a trade office in Reykjavik early in 1957.

Iceland has trade and payment agreements with the following bloc countries: the U.S.S.R., East Germany (Chamber of Foreign Commerce of German Democratic Republic and Icelandic Barter Association), Czechoslovakia, Poland, Rumania, and Hungary. In general, these agreements have been fulfilled.

Yugoslavia

Because of its key geographical position between East and West, and its experiences following expulsion from the Cominform in 1948, Yugoslavia avoided too extensive economic dependence on the Soviet bloc. However, it has not yet achieved that point of economic development where it can maintain a safe balance-of-payments position without reliance on extensive foreign aid and credits. Therefore, even since the resumption of economic relations with the Soviet bloc in 1954, it has continued to accept assistance from, and carry on large-scale trade with, the free world.

In the period immediately following World War II, while it was a member of the Cominform, Yugoslavia maintained close economic and trade relationships with the U.S.S.R. and the countries of the Soviet bloc in Eastern Europe. Almost half of its total trade was with the Soviet bloc, and the bloc's share of certain key Yugoslav imports, such as raw cotton, coke and base metals, and manufactures, considerably exceeded 50 percent. Principal exports to the bloc included meat, tobacco, beverages, pyrites, iron ore, and copper.

During the period 1945–48, Yugoslavia contracted investment credits with the bloc totaling $375 million, although only $23.7 million was actually utilized prior to the rupture of relations. Yugoslavia was also a creditor, granting credits totaling $100 million (of which $40 million had been used prior to the break) to Albania, as well as credits in lesser amounts to other bloc countries. Yugoslavia also enjoyed substantial foreign exchange earnings from bloc transit (through the port of Rijeka) and tourist traffic in this period.

Plans laid for a customs union between Yugoslavia and Bulgaria were interrupted by Stalin's opposition and finally laid to rest by Yugoslavia's expulsion from the Cominform in June 1948. Despite the expulsion, trade continued to flow in the second half of 1948 at nearly the same level as during the first half. Trade fell off sharply in the first few months of 1949, however, with the bloc countries failing to fulfill their contractual obligations, according to the Yugoslavs. All trade between Yugoslavia and the Soviet bloc ceased in mid-1949.

The blow dealt to the Yugoslav Five-Year Plan by the rupture was severe; the Yugoslavs at that time were dependent on the bloc (chiefly the U.S.S.R. and Czechoslovakia) for most of their fuel imports, about four-fifths of their fertilizer and pig iron imports, and extensive quantities of rolling stock and other equipment. In 1949 the value of Yugoslav exports fell by one-third.

The break led to a sharp expansion of trade with free-world countries, a rapid rise in defense expenditures, and a modification of the rate of industrialization. The heavy strain on Yugoslav resources was partly alleviated through large-scale economic assistance from the United States, Great Britain, and France. The basic goal of the Soviet economic blockade of Yugoslavia—to reduce it to the same level of political and economic dependence on the U.S.S.R. as the satellite countries of Eastern Europe—was thwarted largely as a result of this aid from the West.

After the death of Stalin in 1953 the new Soviet leadership, recognizing the pivotal Yugoslav position, and willing to admit that the previous Soviet attitude and actions had been mistaken, set about repairing economic relationships with Yugoslavia which had been ruptured as a result of the 1948 break. The trade embargo imposed by Stalin in an attempt to bring the Yugoslavs to heel was lifted. Trade resumed at the end of 1954 on the basis of barter agreements.

Bulganin and Khrushchev's June 1955 visit to Belgrade, designed to patch up political relations, also accelerated the economic *rapprochement*. During 1955 regular trade and payments agreements were concluded with most Soviet-bloc countries and settlements were made of mutual financial claims dating back to the Cominform period. In September 1955 an agreement in principle was reached by which the Soviet Union agreed to extend long-term, low-interest credits to Yugoslavia. In early 1956 Yugoslavia signed implementation protocols with the U.S.S.R. under this agreement and received additional credits from Poland, Czechoslovakia, and East Germany. Trade with the Soviet bloc continued to expand, both relatively and absolutely, even during the period of strained Yugoslav-Soviet relations which followed the Hungarian revolt. The polemics between Belgrade and Moscow over the Hungarian issue, however, led the U.S.S.R. to take the position that it could not until 1961 begin deliveries of equipment for major developmental projects promised under the credits granted in 1955 and 1956. Following an improvement in Yugoslav-Soviet political relations this issue was resolved by an agreement in July 1957, under which the Soviet Union and Yugoslavia fixed a new compromise delivery schedule.

Bloc Credits. Since early 1956, the Soviet bloc has agreed to provide Yugoslavia with credits amounting to $464 million, of which $299 million is to be furnished by the Soviet Union.[1] The Soviet credits include the following: a $110 million line of credit for the purchase of industrial equipment; a $30

[1] Based on figures available as of February 15, 1958.

million gold and hard currency credit; a $54 million credit for the purchase of raw materials, including agricultural products; a joint credit with East Germany of $175 million for the construction of an aluminum combine, in which the Soviet share reportedly amounts to $105 million. Czechoslovakia has granted Yugoslavia two credits: a $25 million credit for consumer goods and a $50 million credit for capital goods. Poland has extended a $20 million credit for the purchase of rolling stock and industrial equipment. All these credits bear 2 percent interest and have a 10-year repayment period. At the beginning of 1958, however, less than half of these credits had been utilized.

Yugoslavia has recently revised its planning policy to give increased emphasis to investments in agriculture and export industries, and the Yugoslav leaders have stated that large industrial projects will in the future be financed mainly by foreign credits. Thus the Soviet-bloc assistance has been primarily utilized for large-scale projects such as an aluminum combine in Montenegro to be financed by the joint Soviet–East German $175 million credit, a fertilizer factory in Pancevo, and a lignite mining combine in the Kosovo-Metohija region to be financed under the $110 million Soviet investment credit. Soviet credits have also aided agriculture—large amounts of Soviet wheat were shipped in the fall of 1956 under the $54 million credit and land reclamation machinery has been delivered under the $110 million investment credit.

Yugoslavia was able to utilize a substantial portion of the Soviet credits, including the entire $30 million gold and hard currency credit, during 1956, but worsening political relations between Belgrade and Moscow following the Hungarian revolt in November of that year brought deliveries under the credits to a standstill. On February 26, 1957, the Yugoslav Foreign Minister complained publicly that the Soviet Union was making "unacceptable" demands for postponement of deliveries under the credits granted a year before. Apparently, the major items involved were deliveries for the aluminum project which the Soviet Union wished to postpone until 1961 or 1962, when the Yugoslavs, under the original agreement, had hoped to have the first stage of the project in operation. Moscow reportedly also withheld deliveries for power plants and two fertilizer factories scheduled under the $110 million investment credit. Soviet stalling on the developmental credits provoked much bitterness in Yugoslavia, where it was interpreted as political pressure.

Under the terms of a protocol of January 28, 1956, the Soviet Union promised to supply a nuclear reactor for a Yugoslav atomic research center; a protocol was signed on February 2, 1957, confirming this agreement. The Soviet Union apparently also delayed in shipping the reactor and it had not yet been delivered by the end of 1957. Yugoslav officials have since stated publicly, however, that it would be operating by September 1958.

The improvement in political relations between Yugoslavia and the Soviet Union in mid-1957 led to an agreement fixing new schedules for delivery of capital equipment under the $175 million aluminum credit. According to the new schedule the aluminum combine will be completed by 1964. This represents a stretchout of 2–3 years from the original 1956 agreement. Agreement was also reached for programing under the $110 million investment credit and work has already begun on a fertilizer factory with an annual capacity of 360,000 tons and a lignite-mining combine (including a thermal power station). Although there have been some delays in equipment deliveries, the Soviet Union is at present apparently fulfilling its credit commitments.

Technical Training. Yugoslavia currently has technical cooperation protocols with most of the bloc countries providing for the exchange of technical information, but the number of bloc technical personnel working in Yugoslavia is probably only about 50. Most of the Soviet technical experts in Yugoslavia are working on investment projects financed by the U.S.S.R. Thus 12 Soviet experts are supervising the construction of the fertilizer factory in Pancevo and some are probably helping to draft the plans for the lignite combine and the aluminum project. A small number are almost certainly overseeing the construction of installations for the Soviet nuclear reactor at the Yugoslav atomic research center.

The technical exchanges planned under the Yugoslav-bloc technical cooperation protocols have been slow in getting under way. Yugoslavia had a bitter experience with a flood of Soviet technicians prior to 1948 and is now apparently determined to keep the exchange of technicians at a modest level and on the basis of reciprocity.

Trade. Even during the period of especially strained Soviet-Yugoslav political relations during early 1957, Yugoslavia's trade with the Soviet bloc continued to flow smoothly. Yugoslav exports to the bloc during the first 10 months of 1957 came to $82 million (25.9 percent of total exports) and imports from that area to $110.4 million (19.5 percent of total imports). Trade with the bloc has been mounting steadily since 1954, both absolutely and relatively. In that year Yugoslav exports to the bloc came to only $6.2 million (2.6 percent of total exports) and imports from that area amounted to $4 million (1.2 percent of total imports).

The Soviet Union is currently by far Yugoslavia's largest trading partner within the bloc. It accounted for 47.5 percent of Yugoslavia's total trade turnover with the bloc during the first 10 months of 1957 and held fourth place among Yugoslavia's world trading partners, behind the United States, Italy, and West Germany. At the end of October 1957 there was a $15 million balance in favor of the U.S.S.R. on current account (1957 commitments are $56 million each way). There was also a $9.4 million balance in Czechoslovakia's favor on its current account (1957 commitments total $33.4 million), much of which was undoubtedly covered by Yugoslav transit services. All other accounts with the bloc countries were approximately in balance.

Primary products and agricultural goods dominate Yugoslav exports to the bloc. In contrast to the pre-1948 situation, Yugoslavia now exports only limited amounts of base metals to the Soviet bloc. There appears to be a continuing bloc demand for Yugoslav products which are not readily marketable in the West. Industrialization has also increased Yugoslav requirements for certain primary products, including raw cotton and petroleum, which can be procured with relative ease from the bloc. In addition, the U.S.S.R. has supplied some wheat and much-needed coking coal. The share of primary products in Yugoslavia's imports from the bloc is now much larger than in 1948, while the share of base metals, manufactures, and machinery is lower.

There is no information available on prices, but it is probable that Yugoslavia has not been accorded special treatment by the bloc countries.

The Soviet-bloc countries participate regularly in Yugoslav trade fairs, such as the Zagreb International Fair. There are also some 50–100 Soviet commercial representatives in Yugoslavia. No other particular trade promotion efforts have been noted.

Since 1955 Yugoslavia has had annually renewed trade and payments agreements with all the Soviet-bloc countries and Communist China. Two features of these agreements warrant special attention: first, all contain commodity quotas, which are not firm commitments but rather targets to be fulfilled to the extent possible; second, the accords generally specify the basis on which prices in contracts concluded under the agreement will be fixed. Yugoslavia has also signed 3-year trade agreements with four bloc countries (Rumania, U.S.S.R., Poland, and Czechoslovakia) which together accounted for 82.9 percent of Yugoslav trade with the bloc during 1956. The tong-term arrangements provide for the annual exchange of certain amounts of basic commodities, thus facilitating the conclusion of annual protocols.

The bloc appears to be fulfilling its trade commitments at a normal rate. By the end of October 1957, it had fulfilled 80.8 percent of its $136.7 million export commitment to Yugoslavia, while Yugoslavia had met 61.5 percent of its $133.3 million commitment to the bloc. It is quite possible that final 1957 trade statistics will disclose that the bloc met its annual target.

Although Yugoslavia's trade with the bloc has been steadily increasing since 1954, the Yugoslavs have been careful not to let it attain the 1948 level, when trade with the bloc constituted almost 50 percent of total Yugoslav trade. Not only are Yugoslav memories of the Cominform blockade still fresh, but since 1948 trade and credit relationships have been established with the free world. Replacement parts for the existing industrial plant, which is based largely on capital imports from the West, are likely to be obtained from that source rather than from the bloc. The Yugoslavs are currently seeking and finding markets for their industrial products in the less developed areas of the free world, such as the Near and Far East. Finally, Yugoslavia incurred a large debt to the free-world countries following the Cominform break, and servicing of this debt will require exports to the West to be maintained at a high level. For these reasons, Yugoslavia appears inclined to increase its trade with bloc countries parallel with, not at the expense of, its trade with the free world.